SOCIAL ACTION
VS.

EVANGELISM

an essay on the contemporary crisis

William
J. Richardson

SOCIAL ACTION VS. EVANGELISM

an essay on the contemporary crisis

William J. Richardson

William Carey Library

533 HERMOSA STREET • SOUTH PASADENA, CALIF. 91030

Library of Congress Cataloging in Publication Data

Richardson, William J   1921-
    Social action vs. evangelism.

    Includes bibliographical references.
    1. Mission of the church. 2. Evangelistic
work. 3. Social action. 4. Church and social
problems. I. Title.
BV601.8.R49   261.8   77-22669
ISBN 0-87808-160-7

In accord with some of the most recent thinking in the aca-
demic press, the William Carey Library is pleased to present
this scholarly book which has been prepared from an author-
edited camera-ready manuscript.

Published by the William Carey Library
533 Hermosa Street
South Pasadena, Calif. 91030
Telephone 213-682-2047

PRINTED IN THE UNITED STATES OF AMERICA

Contents

v

Preface

In recent years there has been a rising tide of interest in evangelism. This welcome phenomenon, however, has served to bring into focus the anti-evangelistic stance of some churchmen, who depreciate evangelism in the interest of being "relevant" to today's needs.

Much is heard today of the "lifestyle of the congregation in mission" and the "missionary structure of the congregation." What has not always been made clear is that these motifs are being used to describe a type of activity aimed chiefly at challenging oppressive societal structures that seem to keep people in poverty and ignorance. There has been a reinterpretation of missions and missionary structures, with little or no place given to evangelism as integral to the definition of mission. This new definition of mission bears in large measure the stamp of the dominance of secularism in much recent theology.

This book seeks to point up the most crucial of these issues. It seeks to examine what has been happening and to assess its meaning for the church.

Many readers will remember Jesse Bader, for many years Secretary for Evangelism of the National Council of Churches. He was, in the broadest sense of the word, an ecumenist, ardent in social concern, but also an *ardent evangelical* who placed evangelism at the heart of the life of the church in America.* His career represents the kind of linking of evangelism and social concern articulated by Evangelicals at Lausanne in 1974. Dr. Bader would be amazed and distraught by the contemporary depreciation of conversion evangelism described above.

   This little volume is affectionately dedicated to Jesse Bader and to all today who seek to keep the church faithful to its Lord and relevant to the needs of the world as envisioned in the Great Commission.

---

* Today Dr. George Hunter, Executive for Evangelism, the United Methodist Board of Discipleship, is advocating unashamed conversion evangelism all across his ten million member communion, as Bader did in his time.

1

Where the Action Is

The new theology, it is said, "cuts the nerve of missionary motive."(1) This statement describes the crisis of missions, in its theoretical aspects, in the past decade and a half. How are we to respond to this appraisal of the situation? Shall we accept it as proper on the grounds that the older conceptions of missions are invalid? Or rather, without defending everything done in the name of missions or abandoning the Lord's mandate to the church, should we not explore again the meaning of his mandate to evangelize the world in relation to the crucial questions posed by the new theology? Such is the aim of this book.

In this chapter we shall examine the implications of recent theological trends for the meaning of evangelism. We shall then begin to put forward our understanding of the meaning and application of the commission to "make disciples of all the nations."

One cannot speak in the singular in referring to the new theology. There have been many theologies in the recent past; but this is no sign of vitality in the discipline. Professor Van A. Harvey has written of the alarming state of "ill health of Protestant theology in America" symptomized by "lack of serious dialogue, the subsequent narcissism (the theology of autobiography) and faddism (the theologies of atheism, hope, play, revolution, and . . . polytheism). . . ." These, he writes, "are all bleak testimony to a pervasive loss of vocation and the breakdown of a once noble intellectual discipline."(2) James I. McCord has described theology as a "shambles." Others have used expressions such as "theological exhaustion, confusion,

trendlessness, outlinelessness" to describe where theology is in
our day.(3)   It is not surprising that in some circles there has
been a corresponding disparity of understanding of the nature of
the church's mission.

Characteristic of much of the theology underlying the new
concept of missions has been the predominance of a secularistic
attitude and an attendant loss of a sense of transcendence.
Theology has been oriented to the secular. This development in
itself would not be so threatening were it not for the fact that
much of the secularity that has affected the life of the church
and its thought about mission has been in the form of a particular
ideology. Secularism as an ideology should be distinguished from
secularization as a phenomenon of history, described below, whose
course can be traced over a span of centuries and whose roots are
to be found in Biblical faith no less than in such developments
as the Reformation, the Enlightenment, and the rise of modern
science.

The secular--the world in its temporal aspects--does not as
such pose a threat to the Christian faith or its propagation.
Biblical faith is predicated on the assertion that God the
redeemer is God the creator and that man, whose true nature is
defined by reference to God, is prince and therefore steward of
the created world. One of the fruits of the spread of the
Biblical message has been to redeem man from bondage to any
aspect of that created order so that a new concept of holiness--
and with it a new concept of freedom--came into being, having as
its counterpart the desacralization of particular structures of
the created world or of society. Thus Lesslie Newbigen can define
secularization from the Biblical standpoint as "man's entering
into the new freedom given to him in Christ, freedom from the
control of other powers, freedom for the mastery of the created
world which was promised to man according to the Bible."(4)

However, it requires little reflection to see what results
when the world in its temporal aspect is taken as the whole of
reality. It is in this aspect--as a reality-defining system--
that secularism has become in our time a factor affecting the
focus of Christian faith, the ways in which faith is stated, and
the church's understanding of its missionary task. Secularism in
this aspect is a "system of belief which in principle denies the
existence or the significance of realities other than those which
can be measured by natural science."(5) Langdon Gilkey uses four
terms to describe secularism as an attitude: naturalism,
temporalism, relativism and autonomy.

These words express an attitude that finds reality in the
temporal flux immediately around us, effectiveness solely
in the physical and historical (or human) causes in that

process, knowledge possible only of that passing flux, and value only in the fulfillment of its moments. This attitude emphasizes the here and now, the tangible, the manipulatable, the sensible, the relative and the this-worldly.(6)

As the prevailing mood of our time secularism functions to provide "basic attitudes to reality, categories of thought, and evaluations of meaning and goodness."(7)

The most obvious result of secularism for Christian thought has been the predominance of temporalism in theology. There is no transcendent reality to which man need refer either for understanding his existence in this world or for defining his obligations within the various relationships he experiences in this world. Three results of this should be noted in particular.

First there has been a crisis of faith within the church. In the face of secularism as a reality-defining agency any meaningful talk about God becomes impossible. Of course, not all meanings of the expression "God is dead" reflect the impact of secularism. In some instances the term represents only a poorly named attempt to rid religious conversation of outmoded, trivial, self-serving concepts of God.(8) It may also refer to a false piety; Ernest Käsemann asserts that whenever Christians "withdraw from the reality" that God claims for His sovereignty they are treating God as dead.(9) But secularism raises the crucial issue whether God can be spoken of at all. Is there any refinement of language that would make God-talk meaningful? The answer has been "No." Secularism raises the challenge whether man any longer needs God. In this case the assertion that God is dead is a declaration of man's presumed independence.

Quite apart from the crisis of faith experienced within the church there is a crisis of faith experienced by secular man in the world. Generally the secularist attitude is optimistic; using the tools of learning, science, and technology, man can build a better life for himself, a better future. This hope has not been fulfilled. In his sense of terror in the face of the future, in the loss of a sense of meaning of life, in his lack of moral capacity to control the technology he creates, in his need for an adequate basis for community, modern secular man witnesses to his need of a transcendent reality that can bring grace, forgiveness, and hope to his life.

Another result of the impact of secularism upon Christian thought has been that Christian theology has been orienting itself to the secular world. Christian discourse normally belongs within the context of the church and its life; for it is here that a commonly accepted faith stands as the basis for dialogue seeking to understand the faith and its implications for

the individual and corporate life of believers. An exception,
of course, is apologetics whose main objective is to set forth
the grounds for faith. But what we have seen in the recent past
is a whole series of theologies seeking to be relevant to the
secular world and in the process accommodating themselves to
that world. It is this phenomenon which leads John Mulder to
ask: "Who Speaks to the Church?" Mulder declares that

> Contemporary theologians . . . have been virtually united
> in their effort to bring theology to bear on the concerns
> of the secular world. This aim has been variously stated,
> implicitly and explicitly; the agenda for theology . . .
> is determined by cultural trends. The audience to whom
> they must speak is the society at large. The language or
> forms theology employs to communicate must be comprehensible
> to a secular culture, no longer familiar with biblical
> terms and alienated from a biblical view of the world.
> The result has been that theology has become increasingly
> divorced from the church. . . .(10)

This manner of doing theology--of addressing it to the secular
world in the terms of that world, but in the name of Christ, was
renounced in the *Hartford Declaration* (Theme 5) as "an attempt to
exploit the tradition without taking the tradition seriously."
Writing in defense of this theme in the *Hartford Declaration*
Peter Berger declares, "I reject the facile way in which the
tradition has been utilized to legitimate this or that contemporary theology."(11)

The third and, from our perspective, most serious result of
the influence of secularism has been a changed concept of the
nature of the Christian mission and specifically a diminution of
the role of evangelism. In reality this is but another aspect of
the crisis of faith mentioned above. At Uppsala, for example,
there was great disappointment expressed by some delegates over
the fact that concern "for the millions who do not know Christ"
was not the center of focus in discussions of the church's
mission today. The lack of such a stated concern was seen as
symptomatic of a "contemporary 'crisis' of faith" in the church
and not due merely to a difference in ways of stating her
mission.(12)

In part the new conception of evangelism has come as reaction
to what were unworthy aims and methods of the past. The list of
objections is lengthy and includes few, if any, items we would
seek to defend.

At times the aim of evangelism has been the restoration of
Christendom--that older vision of society in which the church was
coterminous with the socio-political structure. Christianity was

the cement that bound together the so-called *Corpus Christianum*.
Even when such an objective could not be realized on an inter-
national scale--as it was thought to have been in the Middle
Ages--it could still be applied to individual states, with the
resulting tendency to equate Christianity with the nation (in
our case Christianity and America).(13)

In its foreign aspects missions has at times become an adjunct
of cultural imperialism reflecting an attitude of racial or
cultural superiority and paternalism toward the beneficiaries of
missionary endeavor. Indigenity was denied to newly formed
churches and they were often kept in a state of dependency on
western churches.(14) At home evangelism has often been coupled
with an emphasis upon individual piety with an attendant lack of
concern about the conditions of life and the social structures in
which the believer lives out his commitment to Christ's lordship
over all of life.(15)

If these were the only points at issue the debate over missions
today would never have assumed the proportions or have become as
serious as it has. Mission is now understood in terms which, in
the judgment of many missiologists, amount to a rejection of
evangelism as its integral part.(16) To a great extent this new
understanding reflects the impact of secularism upon Christian
thought in our day.

The goal of mission in this view is humanization--the realization of authentic human existence. "Humanization" means the
transformation of those structures, whether political, social,
or economic, which prevent mankind from experiencing true freedom
and community.(17) The late Professor J. C. Hoekendijk, for
example, defines evangelism as establishing the "shalom," by
which he means, "peace, integrity, community, harmony, and
justice."(18) The divide between this concept and other views
of missions is described by Elmer Homrighausen in these terms:

> The strong emphasis in ecumenical circles on mission as
> the humanizing and liberating activity of the churches,
> often in collaboration with revolutionary movements, has
> caused many Christians to sense that this trend may de-
> emphasize the necessity for and reality of a converting
> experience and a salvatory relation with Jesus Christ.
> Salvation . . . takes place on the horizontal level by
> which man is brought into the abundant life of human
> well being. The social aspects of man's redemption are
> stressed. . . . what shall be done about the two billion
> people in the world who have never heard of Jesus Christ
> and his liberating and humanizing gospel? If the Chris-
> tian mission is conceived in a largely social sense, then
> what about the great commission's command to "make disci-
> ples"?(19)

In this view evangelism is the involvement of the church in
activities that foster the social changes required for humanization. These activities are classified under the term, "presence,"
a concept which includes such things as: (1) the church's witness
to what God is doing in the world, (2) dialogue with the world
aimed at effecting reconciliation, (3) ministries to the everyday
needs of men, (4) involvement in seeking to change social and
political structures.(20) Some would include as part of social
involvement "acts of subversion and disruption" if warranted by
circumstances.(21) The world writes the agenda for the church.(22)

Notably absent from the above statements of the missionary or
evangelistic task are such elements as personal conversion or the
planting of churches.(23) We are left to wonder what would be
the result of this omission were it carried to its logical
extreme. Would there even be a church to hear the mandate to
participate in God's activity in transforming social structures
for the sake of humanization? It seems that the existence of the
church as the agent of mission is taken for granted without
serious consideration of how the church exists at all.

There has been in all this a perplexing lack of clarity of
distinction between the Gospel and providence. The major concern
has been to discover what God is doing in the world today, then
to adjust the structures and program of the church to join God
where the action is. Even one's theology is determined by his
perception of providence--an approach which Frederick Herzog
describes as an emerging "new principle of doing theology. . . .
How do I know what I think until I see what God does?"(24) The
good news is the providential working of God in the world
today.(25) The life, death, and resurrection of Jesus seem to
have become only signals of the kinds of action that may be
expected of God in the world today.

To be sure Christianity must have a doctrine of providence.
It is unfortunate that for so long this doctrine was identified
with Calvinism so that the giving up of The Calvinistic understanding of God's total sovereignty over events meant the
abandonment of belief in providence. Belief in providence does
not mean ability to interpret all God's actions. Indeed, to
rely on providence for faith--that is, to derive faith from our
ability to see God's hand at work--may lead to unbelief. God may
appear to be silent or inattentive to our expectations. Langdon
Gilkey reminds us that

> To depend for our sense of meaning upon the observable
> victory of our human goals is to be easily vulnerable to
> pessimism and despair. There are times in history when
> our confidence in the meaning of life must be grounded
> in faith, and not in observation alone. But here the

naturalist is caught, for in his world there is nothing
but observable progress on which he can found his courage.(26)

Christian belief in providence is grounded (1) in the doctrine of
creation, which implies God's concern for all his creatures, (2)
in the fact of redemption, where God acted to bring men to fellowship, and (3) in the Christian hope, as the consummation of God's
purpose. All these affirmations have as their corollary the
belief that God is working in history, notwithstanding the lack
of success that usually attends our efforts to interpret his
actions.

But the Gospel is more than a signal of God's presence and
action in the world. It is God's electing and redeeming act in
which He called a new humanity into being, charged with carrying
the good news of redemption to the whole world. To blur the distinction between this decisive act of God in Christ and his
subsequent acts of providence is fraught with several dangers.
One is that we cannot be confident of our ability to discern how
God is acting in a given situation; hence our judgments, as
Andrew M. Greeley warns, often reflect a lack of humility. Moreover, says Greeley, to equate the political and social "programs
and policies one supports" with the Gospel "is to engage in
idolatry . . . for such an equation invests a very contingent
series of political stands with the authority of the absolute."
(27)

Furthermore, when providence becomes the focal point for
identifying where the action is in missions serious consequences
result for the church, especially when providence is viewed in
secular terms. One is the loss of the dimension of ultimacy in
understanding the meaning of salvation which, if taken to its
logical extreme, raises doubts about the legitimacy of the whole
Christian enterprise. It also robs the church of a necessary
criterion for measuring its several ministries; for it is in the
perspective of the prior affirmation of God's redeeming action
that the church finds its definition of appropriate actions to
express its concern for men in society. Another danger,
expressed by John Bennett several years ago, is that the church,
regarding itself as a servant community, will "let down its
guard . . . against being possessed by forces that dominate the
present culture" and become "lost in the world."(28) Only by
clearly distinguishing the Gospel by which it lives will the
church preserve the integrity it must have if it is to minister
to the world.

In the preceding we have analyzed the division today over the
subject of evangelism. We have sought to understand the current
crisis as having its roots in the secularist mood which has
pervaded so much of Christian thought, a mood incidentally which

is more prevalent among theologians and church leaders than among
church members themselves.(29) Many dissenting voices, raised
individually and in groups have protested these developments.
Two documents that have appeared in recent years stand out as
examples of this dissent--the *Frankfort Declaration* (1970) and
the *Hartford Declaration* (1975). In some ways the two documents
are dissimilar. The *Frankfort Declaration* is a forthright call
for the renewal of missions along lines determined by Biblical
faith. The *Hartford Declaration* on the other hand disavows being
an attempt to reaffirm orthodoxy. It is a call for a "return to
transcendence"; yet it seeks to expose the assumptions that have
been "false and debilitating to the church's life and work."(30)
Despite the different contexts out of which these documents
emerged they offer markedly similar perceptions of the issues
involved in the present crisis, particularly in the following:

(1) the impact of secularism upon the definition of evangelism,

(2) the limiting of the scope of missions to horizontal relation-
     ships,

(3) the church's listening to the world rather than to the Lord
     for the terms of its mandate,

(4) the restriction of humanization to the improvement of social
     structures without reference to man's relation to God,

(5) the presumption that no meaningful talk about God is
     possible today,

(6) the tendency to minimize differences among religions as
     inconsequential, therefore calling for a new style of
     evangelism,

(7) limiting Christology to an emphasis upon the humanity of
     Jesus,

(8) defining salvation primarily in this-worldly terms.

In their positive aspects both these documents point to the need
for the recovery of the Transcendent--of faith in God who is the
Lord of history and "master of the future."(31)

These and other statements, while not attempting to put forth
uniform positive conclusions, have served to put the finger on
the crucial issue before the church today. The questions (1)
should the mission be defined as evangelism and (2) what forms of
action are encompassed by the term *evangelism* both depend upon our
understanding of the Gospel.

In what follows we are asserting that evangelism is where the
action is. We recognize that not all that has been called
evangelism is worthy of the name. Nevertheless we believe that
evangelism, refined and informed by the witness of the New
Testament, properly defines the mission of the church. This was
Jessee Bader's conviction; anyone aware of his life and service
both in brotherhood and in interchurch activities knows he was
not myopic in his view of Christian responsibility in the
world.(32) Evangelism is proclaiming Christ and persuading men
to become his disciples and responsible members of his church.
(33) The meaning of each important term in this definition is
determined by the content of the good news which focuses on the
person of Jesus Christ as both the act and the revelation of God.

Jesus is the disclosure that God the creator loves the
creature and seeks him for fellowship. Jesus is the disclosure
to man of the nature of his humanity given him in creation.
Jesus is the act of God reconciling man to himself. By calling
man to a renewed relation to God, Jesus releases him from bondage
to the world so that, as prince of God, man may recover his
stewardship of the world. It is in the recovery of man's
stewardship as the fruit of the Gospel that God stakes out his
claim on the world he created. Finally, Jesus is the disclosure
and the promise of the consummation of the purpose of God for
His creation; in him is the focus of Christian hope.

The Gospel is thus a confrontation of man with truth and grace.
In its disclosure of God's nature as creator and of man's nature
as God's creature the Gospel judges man's present status and
action in the world. In the invitation to man to be reconciled
to God and so to participate in the new humanity the Gospel
discloses the grace of God.

The Gospel in calling man to new relation to God thereby
transforms all his relationships. As son of God he is added to
the family of God--the church. Living as God's son in the world
he seeks to inform all relationships with the values and vision
of life vouchsafed to him through the grace of God. Dean E.
Walker reminds us that Christ's authority as an instrument of
God's grace becomes a liberative force for man's life in the
world. He writes: "Man liberated to the authority of Christ can
change the conditions of earthly life into instruments of
creative service to God and fellow man."(34)

We must be faithful to this Word not only for the sake of the
world but for our own sake as well. Only by faithfulness to the
Gospel will the church maintain the integrity of its own life so
that it may give itself in mission to the world.

The Gospel must provide the content and be the criterion of
our mission. The process of evangelism, in both the means it
employs and in its motives, is fraught with many dangers: allow-
ing the church to become merely the church of a given culture,
making evangelism an extension of some form of imperialism--
ethnic, national or ecclesiastical, or using evangelism as the
instrument of sectarian aggrandizement. Despite all the dangers,
despite all the mistakes that have been or will be made, the
Gospel must be proclaimed and men persuaded to become Jesus'
disciples and responsible members of his church.

Evangelism is where the action is.

NOTES

1. John A. T. Robinson, *Difference in Being a Christian Today*
    (Philadelphia, 1972), pp. 53-54.

2. Van A. Harvey, "Whatever Happened to Theology," *Christianity
    and Crisis*, XXXV, 8 (1975), p. 108. Reprinted by permission
    of *Christianity and Crisis*. Cf. Gordon Kaufman, *Ibid.*,
    p. 111. Other theologies could be added to Harvey's list,
    such as process, secular, black, liberation, women's, social,
    relational.

3. Elmer Homrighausen, "The Church in the World," *Theology
    Today*, XXX, 4 (January, 1974), p. 404.

4. Lesslie Newbigen, *Honest Religion for Secular Man* (Phila-
    delphia, 1966), pp. 8-9, 136. Reprinted by permission of
    Westminster Press. Cf. Louis Dupré, "Religion in a Secular
    World," *Christianity and Crisis*, XXVIII, 6 (1968), pp. 74-75;
    Leroy S. Rouner, "Place of Provincialism in Theology,"
    Christianity and Crisis, XXVI, 1 (February 7, 1966), p. 7.

5. Newbigen, *op cit.*, p. 8. Cf. Langdon Gilkey, *Religion and
    the Scientific Future* (New York, 1970), p. 36. On the
    appropriateness of defining secularism as an ideology see
    Fred P. Thompson, Jr., "The Apologetic Task," *Christian
    Educators Journal*, III, 3 (Fall, 1971), pp. 26-27.

6. Langdon Gilkey, "Secularism's Impact on Contemporary
    Theology," *Christianity and Crisis*, XXV, 5 (April, 1965),
    p. 64. Reprinted by permission of *Christianity and Crisis*.

7. *Ibid.* Cf. also Gilkey's "Theology in the Seventies,"
    Theology Today, XXVII, 2 (July, 1970), p. 294.

8. Alvin C. Porteous, *Search for Christian Credibility* (Nashville, 1971), pp. 43-50; Newbigen, *op. cit.*, pp. 58-59. George W. Forell, *Proclamation of the Gospel in a Pluralistic World* (Philadelphia, 1973), pp. 42-43. Gilkey, *Religion and the Scientific Future*, p. 37.

9. Ernest Käsemann, *Perspectives on Paul* (Philadelphia, 1971), p. 37.

10. John Mulder, "Who Speaks to the Church," *Theology Today*, XXX, 2 (July, 1973), pp. 162-163. Reprinted by permission of the author and *Theology Today*. For a similar analysis see Schubert M. Ogden, "Truth, Truthfulness, and Secularity," *Christianity and Crisis*, XXXI, 5 (1971), pp. 55-60; Brevard S. Childs, *Biblical Theology in Crisis* (Philadelphia, 1970), p. 83.

11. Peter Berger and others, "Theological Table Talk," *Theology Today*, XXXII, 2 (July, 1975), p. 190.

12. Norman Goodall, ed., *Uppsala Report* (Geneva, 1968), p. xix.

13. J. C. Hoekendijk, "The Call to Evangelism," Donald A. McGavran, ed., *Eye of the Storm* (Waco, Texas, 1972), pp. 42 ff. Cf. also the section, "Defense and Further Debate," *ibid.*, pp. 259-279; Porteous, *op. cit.*, p. 182; Colin Williams, *Faith in A Secular Age* (New York, 1966), pp. 65-66; Newbigen, *op. cit.*, pp. 17-18, 124-125.

14. E. Homrighausen, "The Church in the World," *Theology Today*, XXIX, 4 (January, 1973), p. 417.

15. David O. Moberg, *Great Reversal* (Philadelphia, 1972), pp. 34-38, discusses the factors that led to the loss of social concern on the part of some "evangelicals."

16. See Donald A. McGavran and Peter Wagner, "Will Nairobi Champion the Whole Man: An Open Letter to the General Secretary of the World Council of Churches," Donald A. McGavran, ed., *Church Growth Bulletin*, XI, 6 (July, 1975), pp. 459-464.

17. Porteous, *op. cit.*, p. 83. Robinson, *op. cit.*, pp. 54-55. Richard Shaull, "Does Religion Demand Social Change," *Theology Today*, XXVI, 1 (April, 1969), p. 9.

18. Hoekendijk, *op. cit.*, p. 47.

19. Elmer Homrighausen, "The Church in the World," *Theology Today*, XXIX, 4 (January, 1973), p. 419. Reprinted by permission of the author and *Theology Today*. See also Ralph Winter, ed., *Evangelical Response to Bangkok* (Pasadena, 1973), for a statement of the response of prominent Evangelicals to the topic: Salvation Today, taken as the theme of the conference sponsored by the Commission on World Mission and Evangelism of the World Council of Churches at Bangkok, 1973.

20. Porteous, *op. cit.*, p. 83. Williams, *op. cit.*, p. 13n.
    Michael Green, *Evangelism in the Early Church* (Grand
    Rapids, 1970), pp. 147-148. McGavran, *Eye of the Storm*,
    p. 65. McGavran believes there is an appropriate context
    for the strategy of "presence," namely, in the indigenous
    church situation, *ibid.*

21. Shaull, *op. cit.*, p. 12.

22. Goodall, *Uppsala Report*, XVII. Williams, *op. cit.*, p. 108.
    Philip Potter, "Renewal in Mission," McGavran, ed., *Eye of
    the Storm*, p. 262. Despite denials to the contrary this
    phrase has come to mean that the "world's programs" become
    the "norms for the Church's activity." See *Hartford
    Declaration*, Theme 10.

23. Hoekendijk, *op. cit.*, p. 49.

24. Frederick Herzog, "Whatever Happened to Theology," *Christi-
    anity and Crisis*, XXXV, 8 (1975), p. 116.

25. Shaull, *op. cit.*, p. 10. Williams, *op. cit.*, pp. 93 ff.
    This tension was expressed in the study section, "Renewal
    in Mission," *Uppsala Report*, p. 38.

26. Langdon Gilkey, *Maker of Heaven and Earth* (New York, (C)
    1959), p. 165. Reprinted by permission of Doubleday and
    Company, Inc. Cf. Newbigen, *op. cit.*, p. 89.

27. Andrew M. Greeley, "Politics and Political Theologians,"
    Theology Today, XXX, 4 (January, 1974), pp. 392-397.
    Reprinted by permission of the author and *Theology Today*.

28. John C. Bennett, "The Church and the Secular," *Christianity
    and Crisis*, XXVI, 22 (December, 1966), p. 296-296.

29. Hugh Kerr, "Time Out," *Theology Today*, XXX, 2 (July, 1973),
    p. 108.

30. Peter Berger and others, "Theological Table Talk," *Theology
    Today*, XXXII, 2 (July, 1975), pp. 189-190.

31. See the statement of Langdon Gilkey, "Theology in the
    Seventies," *Theology Today*, XXVII, 2 (July, 1970), p. 301,
    as one of many individuals voicing this concern. Martin E.
    Marty and Dean G. Peerman, eds., *New Theology No. 7* (New
    York, 1970), devote a volume of essays to the recovery of
    transcendence.

32. Jesse Bader, "The Divine Impetuosity," *Christian Evangelist*,
    LXI, 8 (February 21, 1924), p. 243.

33. Adapted from McGavran, "Essential Evangelism, An Open Letter
    to Dr. Hoekendijk," *Eye of the Storm*, p. 57.

34. Dean E. Walker, "Authority," *Christian Educators Journal*,
    III, 2 (Summer, 1971), p. 4. Cf. Newbigen, *op. cit.*,
    pp. 147-148.

2

Christianization Is Humanization

"The Church's first concern is not with making converts but with making people."(1) This remark by Bishop John A. T. Robinson points to a fundamental issue in the understanding of evangelism today. Either from an inadequate conception of conversion or from a concept of humanization that lacks Christian validation--perhaps from both--the severance of the two concepts is one of the unfortunate aspects of the current situation.

One is inclined in Robinson's case to attribute his rejection of conversion to a carry over of that understanding of establishment Christianity identified as the Church-type by Ernst Troeltsch. Conversion has no significant place in a society where every person from birth is considered part of the Church. Again, this attitude toward conversion may be in reaction to the "bizarre" exercises of certain sect-type churches. Or again, it may be due to a commitment to a type of humanization which makes conversion irrelevant no matter how well it is defined.

In this chapter we are expressing the conviction that conversion--far from being incompatible with humanization--is the most vital aspect of the process of making life truly human. Christianization, which we are defining as evangelism, is humanization. In making this rather bold assertion we recognize the crucial importance of a proper understanding of both concepts.

MEANING OF HUMANIZATION

One's concept of humanization is necessarily tied to his understanding of what it means to be human, what it means to be a
person. It is a question of the nature of man, which is still the
most engaging question of the twentieth century. It is not a
subject that can be handled with facility in a brief treatment
like this. However, we can point to the great divide between the
naturalistic secular view of man and those views which emphasize
the transcendent as an essential dimension for our understanding
the nature of man and his place in the universe. Daniel Callahan
in a recent analysis declares that a "new warfare is now breaking
out," reminiscent of the old warfare between science and religion.
At issue, he declares, are "fundamentally antagonistic conceptions
of human hope and possibility."(2)

Secularism as a reality-defining system views man in purely
natural, temporal terms. Man is the most highly developed and
differentiated animal. He is the product of "blind chance" and
necessity. His behavior is environmentally conditioned. The
secularist says: "We now *know* that human life resulted from pure
chance just as we now *know* human behavior is shaped and determined."
(3) And whatever values there may be to which we must commit ourselves they are values associated with man's survival, attainable
only through the proper application of "objective knowledge" or
through "deliberate efforts . . . to condition human behavior
toward desirable goals." Science is capable "in the end, or
explaining everything human beings need to know or should reason-
ably want to know."(4) Moreover, secular society can so provide
for creature comforts that it can remove from man any anxiety about
his being. Men indeed experience anxiety in the technocratic
society, but the problems are of a sort that the proper application
of technology will solve them. Joseph Haroutunian represents this
attitude as follows:

> . . . there is no anxiety of existence. There are anxieties
> in life; and these can and will be dealt with through know-
> ledge of "how things are" and the power that goes with such
> knowledge.(5)

This view of man and his place in the whole of things is not a
peculiar phenomenon of the twentieth century. In its most important aspects it is Robert Owen "revisited"; such were the views
expressed by the famous philanthropist in his debate with
Alexander Campbell nearly a century and a half ago.

In Owen's view, man's basic nature is in sum nothing more than
the arrangement of the material particles that make up his being.
The "worm and the insect are his kinsfolk," being made "from the
same original stock of materials."(6) What man becomes is

dependent upon circumstances. Hence, man's physical constitution plus the circumstances of his life determine his character--his beliefs, his capabilities, his attitudes and manner of life. Human nature can be changed if the training of infants is undertaken on the basis of "accurate knowledge of the science of the influence of circumstances over human nature."(7) In unbounded optimism Owen describes a society formed on the basis of his twelve "divine laws":

> Under this new dispensation, their character will be so completely changed or new-formed, that, in comparison of what they have been and are, they will become beings of a superior order. . . .
>
> They will be indeed regenerated, for "their minds will be born again" and old things will be made to "pass away and all to become new."(8)

The goal of these social arrangements is man's happiness in this world, there being no other world for man to look to. Education will aim at helping men to "give a faithful expression of their sensations."(9) The only and proper aim of man is the perfecting of life in this world. In the society Owen envisions there will be no anxiety.

> They will no longer vainly expend their time and faculties upon imaginary future existences which belong not to their nature; but they will at once apply themselves, heart and soul, to make a paradise of their present abode, that each generation in succession may enjoy it continually without any ignorant fears of the future. . . .(10)

On its positive side Owen's program calls for settling the conditions and structures of society to foster the development of its members to the full potential of their natural organization. On its negative side Owen's program seeks to eradicate those institutions which by their very structure inhibit the full realization of man's potential. These institutions are artifical laws, government, private property, marriage, and, of course, religion.(11)

Owen's program, although revolutionary in conception was not immoderate in its visualization of means. Himself a gentle person and confident of the basic rationality of people, he did not advocate a violent transition from the old to the new order. Persons displaced by the doing away of the old order--the clergy, for example--should not be made to suffer in the process. They too were products of circumstance and for this they should receive no blame.

We must allow for a certain naivete in Robert Owen; he had imbibed rather freely at the fountain of romanticism. We must also allow for the difference between his times and our own. Nevertheless his views closely resemble much that has been advocated in the name of humanization not only by secular human- ists, which we would expect, but by some theologians as well. We note the following points of similarity between Robert Owen and contemporary secular theology.

(1) The nature of man is understood almost completely within the limits of his temporal existence. In some instances this has reached the point where the New Testament picture of Jesus no longer serves as a paradigm of the "new humanity."(12)

(2) As a corollary of this view of man "salvation . . . takes place on the horizontal level."(13) It consists in the realization of human potential. "The question of hope beyond death is irrelevant or at best marginal to the Christian under- standing of human fulfillment."(14)

(3) Modern science and technology hold forth the promise that man may realize his goals without dependence upon God. Human achievement is the counterpart of the death of God.(15)

(4) "Individual self-realization and human community" are the identifying marks of what it means to be truly human.(16) Whatever alienates men from each other or denies them freedom is dehumanizing.

(5) Hence the means to humanization is freeing people from "institutions and historical traditions"(17) through political and social action. This action will include resistance to oppressive institutions as well as seeking to achieve "greater justice, freedom, and dignity."(18)

These developments, which Langdon Gilkey sees as the impact of secularism upon contemporary theology, have their roots in efforts to "relate the biblical God to a naturalistically interpreted process."

It is not surprizing that at this point a "religionless Christianity" should appear powerfully in our midst, a Christianity that seeks to understand itself in some terms other than man's dependence upon God, and to realize itself totally in the "secular," in the service to the neighbor in the world. The end result has been the appearance of the "God is dead" theologies, which openly proclaim the truth of the new secularity described above, reject . . . all language about God, and in a thoroughly secular way concentrate on life and action in the modern world. . .(19)

It must seem like mistaken, if not unfair, categorizing to
lump together secular humanists and "secular" theologians who
are proclaiming humanization in the name of Christ. Surely the
charge of "atheism" does not fit all of the latter. What seems
to be the case is that many theologians, for a variety of
reasons, have relinquished too much ground to the secularists,
with the result that both their definition of the goal and their
model of humanization differ in no significant respect from
those of the secularists.

A chorus of voices joins in expressing this perception of the
effect of the secularist outlook on the nature of man and his
life in the world; and they are not voices from the far right
only. Professor Homrighausen, as we have seen, identifies this
issue as the current crisis in missions.(20) This was the
concern of the eighteen original signers of the *Hartford Declaration*--Protestant, Roman Catholic, Orthodox. One of the principal
organizers of the Hartford meeting, Richard John Neuhaus, in a
debate sponsored by the Faith and Order Commission (NCC) made the
following remark about the intention of the signers of the
declaration:

> We are saying that an awful lot of contemporary theology--
> right, left, and center--has indeed become anthropology,
> that it is no longer in tension with, in dialectial rela-
> tionship to the referent which we call God, the Transcen-
> dent which keeps it under judgment.(21)

President James I. McCord expresses a similar view, declaring
that the church has witnessed "a capitulation to forms of
secularity that differed little from bald secularism."(22) Moreover, studies like that of Dean M. Kelly, *Why Conservative
Churches Are Growing*, indicate that many church members also
share this judgment, sensing an erosion of "structures of meaning"
and the disappearance of "theological direction."(23)

It will become evident as we proceed that we do not find in
the Christian faith any encouragement for a lack of concern for
man's life in the world. The Word who called all things into
being and who became incarnate in Christ Jesus witnesses to the
reality and validity of creaturely existence. What we are
objecting to is the debilitating result of a purely horizontal
view of man and his life in the world. The words of William
Ernest Hocking, notwithstanding his disparagement of evangelical
missions, best describe this result.

> . . . if the final state of things gives us the lasting
> sum of their values, we can hardly avoid the reflection
> of Tolstoi that an ultimate annihilation sends its shadow
> backward and cancels the worth of every present achieve-
> ment.(24)

The secularist perspective of the nature of man, when it is
associated with human efforts to shape the future, is self-
contradictory; its view of man's nature is deterministic while
its concept of man's responsibility for the future is voluntar-
istic. This contradiction, Langdon Gilkey reminds us, appears
in the two roles of science today. In its first role science is
"a body of conclusions, theories, or hypotheses about the nature
and interrelations of things, including man." In its second role
it serves "as a magnificent act of human creative rational
autonomy . . . a means through which scientific man exercises a
newfound control over his world, including his own species."
Herein lies the contradiction:

> the *knowledge* science produces . . . moves our thought
> about man in the direction of total determinism, while
> . . . the creative enterprize or *activity* of science
> . . . moves our thought about man inevitably toward empha-
> sizing human freedom. . . . when this view of man as a
> determined object is taken as an exhaustive explanation
> or description of man, it makes absurd and unreal the
> very language its perpetuators employ about the *uses* of
> this same knowledge.(25)

This same contradiction appears in Robert Owen. On the one
hand he sees man as determined, as the product of his physical
constitution and character-shaping circumstances; man cannot "by
his will . . . control his belief and his conduct."(26) Yet,
says Owen, it is the "duty of man . . . to find out the laws of
his nature, that he may first know what manner of being he is,
and then form all his institutions . . . in strict accordance
with these divine laws."(27) The same contradiction appears
currently in the program of B. F. Skinner, who discards all talk
about responsibility "as a myth," yet the advocates of his
position exhort "the rest of us to voluntarily concur in their
views."(28)

Moreover, we have to ask whether secularism as a world view
can give adequate support for the value it places upon survival
or upon the significance of persons. Why, being a product of
blind chance, should humanity survive? On what grounds if the
significance of persons affirmed? These questions have been
raised many times. The issue was expressed most succinctly by
Denison Maurice Allan in the James Sprunt Lectures three decades
ago:

> Many of the most learned thinkers of our day--John Dewey,
> Ernst Cassirer, G. E. Moore, and Nicolai Hartmann--
> starting with different points of view, have ended up
> with this paradox: they cherish the high values of human
> personality as truly valuable but cannot find any cosmic

support for them in a Supreme Person. As they see it,
man's aspirations toward ideal goodness, beauty, and truth
have just mysteriously emerged from nature's strange fertility without guidance and without design. Yet they con-
stitute a worshipful addendum to the sum of nature's works.
How can values be *normatively* objective and *genetically*
subjective?(29)

An accompaniment of this lack of adequate ground for asserting
human worth are the dangers associated with the secularist
vision of *goals* and *means* in the shaping of the future of man.
The secularist envisions the fulfillment of creaturely needs in
society and within history; in that fulfillment men will have no
cause to be anxious. This denial of any anxiety other than that
pertaining to temporal needs is itself a denial of humanity. Men
are anxious about food and raiment, but they also experience
anxiety at a much deeper level. Tillich called this anxiety the
concern with the question of being. Joseph Haroutunian sees the
question of being as heightened by the fact that as human beings
we experience love.

> Anxiety is a function of the transactions which constitute
> human life. We are anxious when and as we love people and
> things who transact with us, because both people and
> things disappear and we also shall disappear. . . .
> Anxiety is a function of love . . . where love is there
> must also be anxiety.(30)

However defined, this deeper aspect of anxiety is a mark of
being human and the denial of it is dehumanizing in its tendency.
This issue likewise appeared in Mr. Campbell's debate with Owen.
In Owen's view, says Campbell, "man, at *his* zenith, is a stall-
fed ox." To assume that "when, like an ox, he has eated and
drank [sic] his fill, then he is happy" is to "degrade man."(31)

Another danger is that secularist attempts to form the future
may involve the use of means that are totalitarian. This may
result from the mistaken optimism that scientific method—so
magnificent in its achievements in the control of nature—could
suffice as an instrument for the control of man in society. The
exercise of this kind of control, Gilkey says, may become
tyrannical and dehumanizing.

> A strictly "scientific" view of man and his destiny, taken
> seriously, might tend to regard society as a vast labora-
> tory, in which only the scientific manipulator and his
> political bosses retain their freedom.(32)

CHRISTIAN VIEW OF HUMANIZATION

We have devoted the larger portion of our remarks to a description of humanization from the assumptions of secularism. The question to be asked now is: To what alternative do we appeal in the name of evangelism?

On Biblical grounds we must reject an approach to humanization that denies validity to the believer's existence in this world, that appeals only to the otherworldly for the meaning of the truly human. This is what occurs when the objective of evangelism is expressed solely in terms of "saving souls."(33) This attitude presumes a partial view of man: the "soul" is the basic reality with which the Gospel is concerned. The body is either rejected as inimical to the spiritual life (a misunderstanding of "flesh") or merely tolerated as having no significance to it.(34) The New Testament supports no such concept of man's nature and purpose in this world. It is also a misunderstanding of the injunction: "Love not the world . . ." (I John 2:15). What is opposed in this epistle is making the world the sum of reality and its values, which is idolatry. But the opposite of idolatry is not rejecting the world but the proper stewardship of it. Hence the "otherworldly" understanding of our humanity in effect denies God's claim on the world and is thus a denial of the truly spiritual.

The fact of the matter is that a proper Christian approach to understanding man does recognize the material and biological aspects of his life. It recognizes also the social and political dimensions of his life in community, although it does not attempt to provide a model for a normative social and political order. The Christian view does not reject the material as evil. It too is created. Man can participate in its structures as an act of stewardship. But the Christian approach recognizes another dimension as essential to the understanding of humanity, that is, a relationship to Him who is the source and ground of man's existence. It insists that in the absence of the dimension of fellowship with God the other dimensions lack meaning and are susceptible to distortion--either through idolatry, where the created claims man's loyalty, or through loss of stewardship, where the created is misused. Is this not the meaning of the Biblical concept that it is man's estrangement from God that leads to distortion in all other relationships of life? (Romans 1:18-30)

What we are saying here is brilliantly expressed in Denison M. Allan's lecture, "Rival Views of Personality." Here he describes three basic approaches for understanding man: the Naturalistic view (the physical and biological dimensions), the Humanistic interpretations (conscious, social, and political dimensions),

and the Transcendental views of man (the dimension of reason, the
dimension of creative growth, and the eternal dimension). The
whole truth about man, Professor Allan contends, lies not in any
one of these views apart but in all three of them taken together.
By what he calls the eternal dimension Allan means "human personality in the image and potential likeness of God." This new
dimension of personality, says Allan,

> . . . is not an architectural addition to our natural life.
> It is rather a reorganization of the whole being on a
> radically new plan. That is why it is spoken of as a new
> birth or as entering into life. . . . This new realm of
> being comes neither from the potentialities of man's
> spirit alone, nor from the Divine Personality alone, but
> from a creative relationship between the two.(35)

This relationship of man and God does not stand over against the
other relationships man experiences in the world; it is rather
the potential for bringing these relationships into meaningful
harmony.

This integrative aspect of faith in God is the point of Jan M.
Lockman's analysis of the points of convergence and divergence
between Christianity and Marxism. Christianity and Marxism are
alike (1) in viewing man as a social creature, (2) in taking
history seriously, and (3) in thought oriented to the future.
The chief point of divergence between them is the Gospel which
proclaims the incarnation of God. "The Christian message draws
men into the discipleship of Jesus of Nazareth and then into *his*
history, society and future. . . . the final point of reference
of this man is God." What happens to man, then, when life is
robbed of this perspective?

> If God is ideologically denied, then man is threatened to
> become dissolved in his history, society and his future
> and he becomes imprisoned in his immanence and in his
> worldly projects. The penultimate becomes the ultimate
> for him.(36)

The christian contention is that only in the light of fellowship
with God can man find meaning and direction for the expression of
his personal propensities and his participation in all the relationships open to him in the world.

In Biblical terms authentic humanity is rooted in God's
creation of man for fellowship. On this base rests the assertion
of the goodness and value of the material world. In this light
man may understand his creaturely existence as purposeful--there-
fore meaningful--and hopeful in the expectation of the consummation
of fellowship. Made in the image of the Creator he participates

(1) in relation to others, and so enjoys community, and (2) in
relation to things, and so fulfills his stewardship. He is not
self-existent, therefore his true humanity consists in meaningful
relationship to God.

But man, created for fellowship, possesses a freedom that is
real though not absolute. He may exercise his will in revolt.
Desiring structures of security for his life, he seeks to establish his life on his own terms apart from God--but with the means
God has provided. Thus estranged from God he experiences dis-
orientation in the whole of his existence. He lacks inner
harmony; his life in community is distorted; his sense of stewardship is lost and he becomes an exploiter of the world. This is
dehumanization and its root is in "man's revolt against God."(37)

The Gospel is God's word of truth and grace. As the word of
truth it confronts man with his loss of true humanity as the
fruit of his estrangement from God. As the word of grace it sets
before man the way to normal existence through restoration to
sonship in new birth.

With Donald A. McGavran we have defined evangelism as proclaiming Christ and persuading men to become his disciples and
responsible members of his church. This definition of evangelism
contains three elements: (1) proclaiming Christ, (2) persuading
men to become his disciples, and (3) responsible membership in
his church. The question now is: What have these elements to
do with humanization?

The proclamation of Christ asserts that he is the disclosure
of God in his nature as love and his purpose to reconcile man to
himself. Jesus is also the disclosure to man of the true meaning
of his creatureliness. He is the Savior who brings wholeness to
man's life by uniting him with God in true sonship. He is the
model of the eschatological fulfillment of true humanity. "We
shall be like him for we shall see him as he is." (I John 3:2)

Persuading men to become his disciples is calling them to new
existence "in Christ." In baptims one accepts God's judgment on
his old life and God's grace for a new life. He puts off the old
nature and puts on the new nature "renewed in knowledge after the
image of Him that created him." (Col. 3:10) His participation in
the new humanity is the basis for his moral life. It is the basis
for the new unity among men; in Christ "there is neither Greek nor
Jew . . . Barbarian, Scythian, bond or free, but Christ is all,
and in all." (Colossians 3:11) It is, moreover, the basis for
appropriate action in the world and in all the relations in which
he takes part in day to day life. (Colossians 3:5-4:6) In Christ
man recovers his stewardship. Salvation does not mean ones
removal from the world but rather a movement into the world as
the scene of his obedience to God.

The church is the community of the new humanity--the chosen
people of God in pilgrimage to their appointed inheritance. But
it is not an exclusive community. When it is true to itself this
fellowship transcends and overcomes the limits of the structures
of community in the world. By faithfulness to its Lord the
church both experiences and overcomes the tension of particularity.
The church's confession of the risen Lord is the mark of its
particularity; by its obedience to the mandate of the risen Lord
the church witnesses to its understanding that what the Lord has
done in making the church the people of God is in reality his
intention for the whole world. The church thus has a double
obligation: to be faithful to its identity as the people of God
and to be God's instrument of service to all men in terms of the
verdict of their worth declared in the Cross of Christ. The
church is the new humanity calling upon all men to share the
blessings of the Father's house.

Christianization--as the winning of people to this allegiance--
is humanization.

In his recent study of the New Testament ordinances Vernard
Eller discusses the meaning of baptism as the receiving of the
Holy Spirit. The coming of God into the life of the believer,
which Eller identifies as the Holy Spirit, is

. . . not to be understood as an exceptional event happening to exceptional people--a mysterious breaking in of the
divine. It is becoming human--according to the definition
of the one who invented human beings in the first place.

. . . Baptism, as the receiving of the Holy Spirit, is
another presentiment of our humanity. And the mood during
the service is not to be "Thank God, our brother has found
the fire escape," but "Glory be! Kingdom come! It's
happening. The race is finally on its way to getting
human; our brother just decided to let God make a man out
of him!"(38)

NOTES

1. Robinson, *Difference in Being a Christian Today*, p. 58.

2. Daniel Callahan, "Faith and Reason and Survival," *Christianity
   and Crisis*, XXXII, 10 (July, 1972), p. 175.

3. *Ibid.*, p. 176.

4. *Ibid.*

5. Joseph Haroutunian, "The Question Tillich Left Us," Nels F.
    S. Ferré et al, *Paul Tillich, Retrospect and Future*
    (Nashville, 1966), p. 56. Reprinted by permission of
    Abingdon Press.

6. Robert Owen and Alexander Campbell, *Evidences of Christianity,
    Debate*, new ed. (St. Louis, 1906), p. 161.

7. *Ibid.*, p. 27.

8. *Ibid.*

9. *Ibid.*, p. 129.

10. *Ibid.*, p. 162.

11. *Ibid.*, pp. 115-118.

12. Richard Shaull and Barbara Hill, "Somewhere Along the Road,"
    Theology Today, XXIX, 1 (April, 1972), pp. 96-98. Porteous,
    Search for Christian Credibility, pp. 117-140, presents what
    he calls "Images of Christ for a Secular Age."

13. Elmer Homrighausen, "The Church in the World," *Theology Today*,
    XXIX, 4 (January, 1973), p. 419.

14. *Hartford Declaration* (Themes 6 and 13), reprinted in *Theology
    Today*, XXXII, 1 (April, 1975), pp. 94-97.

15. George Forell, *Proclamation of the Gospel in a Pluralistic
    World*, pp. 42-43.

16. *Hartford Declaration* (Theme 8).

17. *Ibid.* (Theme 9).

18. Philip Potter, "Renewal in Mission," Donald A. McGavran, ed.,
    Eye of the Storm, p. 263. Cf. also Daniel L. Migliore,
    "Biblical Eschatology and Political Hermeneutics," *Theology
    Today*, XXVI, 2 (July, 1969), pp. 123-131; Porteous, *op. cit.*,
    pp. 63-91

19. Langdon Gilkey, "Secularism's Impact on Contemporary Theology,"
    Christianity and Crisis, XXV, 5 (April, 1965), p. 65.
    Reprinted by permission of *Christianity and Crisis*.

20. Homrighausen, "The Church in the World," *Theology Today*,
    XXXIX, 4 (January, 1973), p. 419.

21. Richard John Neuhaus, William Sloan Coffin, Jr., and Harvey
    Cox, "The Hartford Debate," *Christianity and Crisis*, XXV, 12
    (July 21, 1975), p. 174. Reprinted by permission of
    Christianity and Crisis. Cf. Peter Beyerhaus, *Missions,
    Which Way* (Grand Rapids, 1971), pp. 86-87.

22. James I. McCord, "Three Decades Later," *Theology Today*, XXX,
    2 (June, 1974), p. 324. Cf. also John Bennett, "The Church
    and the Secular," *Christianity and Crisis*, XXV, 22 (December
    26, 1966), pp. 294-297.

23. *Ibid.*

24. William Ernest Hocking, *Meaning of Immortality in Human Experience*, rev. ed. (New York, 1958), p. 10. Reprinted by permission of Harper and Row.

25. Gilkey, *Religion and the Scientific Future*, pp. 82-83. Reprinted by permission of Harper and Row.

26. Owen and Campbell, *op. cit.*, p. 185.

27. *Ibid.*, p. 163.

28. Karl Menninger, *Whatever Became of Sin* (New York, 1973), pp. 78-79.

29. Denison Maurice Allan, *Realm of Personality* (Nashville, 1947), p. 47.

30. Haroutunian, "The Question Tillich Left Us," *Paul Tillich, Retrospect and Future*, pp. 60-61. Reprinted by permission of Abingdon Press.

31. Owen and Campbell, *op. cit.*, pp. 389-390.

32. Gilkey, *Religion and the Scientific Future*, pp. 86-87. Reprinted by permission of Harper and Row. Cf. Newbigen, *Honest Religion*, pp. 62, 76; Dean E. Walker, *Authority of the Word* (Milligan College, 1950), p. 5.

33. Moberg, *Great Reversal*, pp. 55-56.

34. See Käsemann, *Perspectives on Paul*, pp. 114-115, on the significance of the human body.

35. Allan, *op. cit.*, pp. 48-49.

36. Jan M. Lockman, "Christianity and Marxism: Convergence and Divergence," *Christianity and Crisis*, XXIX, 8 (May 12, 1969), pp. 131-133. Reprinted by permission of *Christianity and Crisis*.

37. Forell, *op. cit.*, p. 26. Cf. Gilkey, *Maker of Heaven and Earth*, p. 220.

38. Vernard Eller, *In Place of Sacraments* (Grand Rapids, 1972), pp. 54-55. Reprinted by permission of Eerdmans.

3

Evangelism
Is Social Action

Fifty years ago Jesse Bader wrote: "The way to Christianize the social order is to Christianize folks and the way to Christianize folks is one by one. . . . Evangelism is the divine quest of the individual for God."(1) Only a few years before Mr. Bader, then Secretary of Evangelism for the American Christian Missionary Society, had laid out a five-year goal of one million baptisms in the Christian Churches.(2) Jesse Bader believed evangelism is the way to change society. Our purpose in this chapter is to examine this concept of Christian involvement in the affairs of the world.

The relation of the people of God to the society surrounding them has always been a problem for the church. The roots of the problem go deeper than the often inadequate perceptions believers have of their relation to the world. It lies in the fact that believers, while still being part of humanity itself, are the new humanity. Both of these facts of existence represent relationships whose responsibilities are hard to define.

Man in the Biblical perspective is among other things a social creature. He has a stewardship that he is to fulfill through relationship with others at different levels of involvement; and he has needs that are fulfilled only in relationship with others. Dean Arthur Glasser speaks of a "cultural mandate" existing for man from the beginning.

The commands of [Genesis 1, 2]. . . mark the beginning of a stream of obligation, a mandate for family and community,

law and order, culture and civilization, that widens and
deepens as it courses through Scripture. By it God calls
all men to the role of vice-regents over this world; all
are to participate responsibly in this task.(3)

Surely there is what may be legitimately called a "social concern"
deriving from these necessary relationships and obligations in
which all men share as part of the human race.

The Biblical perspective focuses upon another social relationship, namely that of the covenant community drawn from the world
in response to God's elective grace. This community is not
coterminous with mankind in general but is nevertheless identified
with the whole of mankind in a peculiar way because of its
mission; ". . . the people of God who listen for his Word, who
obey his commandments and who seek his presence in worship are in
principle the whole of humanity."(4)

In its life the covenant community experiences tension arising
from this dual relationship and the responsibilities that
accompany it. This was as true for the Old Israel as it is for
the New Israel, though perhaps in different ways. On the one
hand the church must maintain its integrity in its covenant
relationship so that it may fulfill God's purpose for it. At
the same time the church cannot be lacking in concern for matters
in the world around it or be unrelated to that world. This two-
fold obligation has its roots in the Biblical conception of God
as both creator and redeemer. "In Christ," says Lesslie Newbigen,
"the Christian learns both to deny and to affirm the world--to
deny it in its self-sufficiency, to affirm it as the object of
God's love."(5)

A second tension for the people of God appears in the realm of
ethical norms. The Christian, believing that the Lord who lays
claim on his obedience is the Lord of all, must regard the norms
given for his life as applicable to all men. However, since
these norms have their basis in the assertion: "Thus says the
Lord," the binding force of these particular norms rests upon the
prior decision to bring one's life under the Lord's authority.
Brevard Childs warns us that to translate Biblical imperatives
"into ethical norms for society in general runs the acute danger
of impairing the radical newness of the Gospel which provides the
sole ground for an obedient life before God."(6)

A third area of tension exists wherever the new relationship
into which one is drawn by acceptance of Christ conflicts with
certain of the political or social structures of the wider
community of which he is part. For example, the Christian faith
is not committed to a particular political structure as the
counterpart of the Gospel. If, however, the Christian is cast

into a situation where a divinized political structure demands
loyalty belonging only to God his choice to obey God becomes in
part a political decision. If the church, in heeding the command
of the Lord, identifies itself with those whom a society has
dispossessed, this act of identification becomes a judgment upon
the dispossessors. Thus the people of God may experience tension
between their obedience to God and the expectation of the society
of which they are a part. Further, the church may experience the
sufferings of Jesus as it fulfills its loyalty to God.(7)

How then does the Christian community express the concern it
shares with all men for how things are in the world while still
communicating the Christian values which it believes pertain to
all men? The church cannot sit back and await the hoped-for time
when all men have accepted God's call to live by the terms of the
covenant; it must contend for those values now. Yet the church
knows that its vision of life and the values corresponding to
that vision are built upon covenant faith and have their sanction
in that faith; addressing those values to society apart from the
context of the covenant may become a betrayal of that faith.

Too often the church attempts to make responses that avoid the
tensions described above. These attempts and their results are
described by Suzanne De Dietrich as follows:

> Two temptations constantly threaten the witnessing commu-
> nity. One is to consider the separate life as an end in
> itself. This produces a ghetto religion, the self-
> righteousness of the Pharisee, the exclusiveness of the
> "saved." The other is to succumb to a slow process of
> assimilation by which God's People lose their identity
> and adopt the way of life of the pagan or secular civili-
> zation which surrounds them.(8)

A church may be separatist when it stresses only the "private"
morality of its members, taking no account of their obligation
within the structures of life in the society of which they are
part.(9) The separatist approach often appears under the guise
of being neutral on social problems. But the neutralist, however
sincere he may be in taking this position, cannot avoid the
appearance of standing with the side that wins out on a particular
issue. Moreover, the injunction: "Be not conformed to this
world" (Romans 12:2) implies a need to be aware of ways the world
impinges upon the believer's life plus the determination that
one's stance in every relationship of life reflect his obedience
to God.(10)

The tendency toward assimilation--the absorption of the people
of God into the surrounding culture--has had a variety of manifes-
tations. In one of its earliest forms it appeared in that

concept of society known as Christendom. In theory the church
was not subservient to culture; in Theory the "two swords"
doctrine safeguarded the church from the intrusions of the
secular and provided structures by which the church could influence public policy. In the end, however, the church did become
subservient. Its critical role was weakened and ineffectual.

Culture-Protestantism, which interpreted the values of the
Gospel in cultural terms, is another instance of assimilation.
It made the Kingdom of God synonymous with the brotherhood of
man. Its goal was peace and brotherhood in a "perfected social
order"(11) to be realized through the application of the Christian ethic to the barious institutions and structures of society
by persons following the leadership of Jesus. By its alliance
with the world, culture-Protestantism removed the scandal of
Christ and his cross and in the process lost the authority that
stands in judgment and grace over all the endeavors of men.

Strange as it may seem, the current advocacy of active involvement of the church in changing social and political structures
tends toward the result of assimilating the church in secular
culture despite its intentions to the contrary. According to
this approach, God's action in the world is directed toward the
elimination of bondage and injustice. As the church discovers
where the action is it throws its resources into the struggle.
In this concept of mission the church tends to be united more by
its commitment to making social changes than by its commitment
to the God of the covenant. It is thus threatened with the loss
of its integrity. Such is the fear of Professor John C. Bennett.
The current emphasis upon the church as the "servant church" may
result in the church becoming what he calls "merely an echo" of
the very structures to which it ministers.(12)

One still hears talk about the prophetic role of the preacher
in society after the manner of the prophets of Israel. But this
identification can only be made on the assumption of the Old
Testament theocracy as the model for the relation of church to
society today. Much recent thought, such as described above,
seems incipiently to assume this modality. Our society, however,
is a pluralistic and secular society, quite unlike that of Old
Testament Israel, which was both a nation and a church. It was
this fact that made it possible for Nathan the prophet to point
the finger at David the king and say: "Thou art the man." (II
Samuel 12:7) To assume this kind of prophetic role for the
preacher in today's world is to imply a concept of society as a
re-establishment of the *Corpus Chrstianum*. Moreover, it means
the demythologization of the Old Testament prophets by reducing
their message to the level of our contemporary insights.(13)

How then can the church avoid accommodating itself to the world on the one hand or evading its responsibility to the world on the other? Several options commend themselves to our thinking. One of these is the theme of this lecture. Another, which we will affirm but treat only briefly, is the serious involvement of believers in the various structures of life in the world. Such involvement can result in positive changes in these structures. The church can motivate and sustain such participation by its members; but it must recognize their need of the undergirding of faith for this purpose.(14)

Not enough attention has been given to the congregation as the locus for the inspiration and guidance of individual believers in their obedience to God in all relationships of their lives.(15) Indeed, some believe that leaving to committed Christians the task of effecting changes in the social and political order is a retreat from responsibility by the church. If this approach has not always succeeded it is because the church has failed to edify its members to the implications of their life in the world as members of Christ. "Ye are bought with a price, therefore, glorify God in your body." (I Corinthians 6:20) It may be that efforts to exert corporate pressure to change society have encouraged individual believers to feel they are not responsible to bring the Gospel to bear upon every area of their lives.

Andrew M. Greeley, whose views on this subject are the more significant because he is a Roman Catholic sociologist and theologian, holds that the actions of individual believers can be more effective than corporate actions, especially in politics. He questions whether the church possesses the needed competence. He asks: "How can it [the church] take a stand that is both informed and responsive to the insights of all its members?" He envisions the role of the believer as follows:

> Christians, informed by the religious vision provided by the Christian symbol system, and competent in the various technical and political skills that are necessary, may very well engage in theologically enforced politics.(16)

There is reason to believe that this approach, if valid in the sphere of politics, will be valid in other spheres of action by Christians as well.

We have said that by evangelism the church can relate to the world in a positive way while avoiding the two pitfalls of separatism and assimilation. We have gone a step further to assert that evangelism is social action! Can we make this assertion without dissolving the distinction between evangelism and edification, without dissolving the distinction between evangelism and welfare--feeding the hungry, healing the sick?

Can this assertion be made without requiring evangelism to mean
direct involvement in changing social, political, economic
systems? These are serious questions. We believe they can be
answered affirmatively. Social involvement is not merely a
legitimate addendum to evangelism. Evangelism itself, in faithfulness to its Biblical mandate, is social action.

The crisis in missions today, as we have noted already, is
over the question whether social and political action can replace
evangelism as the focus of the task of Christians. At the same
time those who stress evangelism as the proper mission of the
church have forthrightly declared that as an accompaniment of
evangelism Christians have the duty to be involved in socio-
political matters. Theme 5 of the Lausanne Covenant (1974)
affirms this obligation while setting forth its view of the
current crisis:

> Although reconciliation with man is not reconciliation
> with God, nor is social action evangelism, nor is political
> liberation salvation, nevertheless we affirm that evangel-
> ism and socio-political involvement are both part of our
> Christian duty.(17)

In what follows we do not seek to reduce the terms of this
crisis, which is so serious it threatens to produce further
division in the churches.(18) We do suggest, however, that there
is an even more positive relation between evangelism and social
action; we suggest that there may be an understanding of social
action that is implicit to evangelism properly understood. We
have become so accustomed to the concept of social action as
social engineering or as the application of political pressure
in the name of Christ that we are not quite prepared to see that
bringing men to a saving relationship to God in Christ is itself
action that aims at the transformation of all other relationships.
It is social action. To this proposal we address ourselves in
what follows.

1. Evangelism takes place in a social context--at the Temple
in Jerusalem, at a synagogue in Iconium, or in a chariot enroute
from Jerusalem to Gaza. The Gospel interacts with that context.
The interaction does not follow a specific pattern. It cannot be
regularized, and it is important to remember this. The given
element in each case is the Gospel; the nature of the interaction
varies with the situation. For example, the social context may
involve an audience that is a mixture of races and of sexes. At
Iconium the converts of Paul and Barnabus were both Jews and
Greeks (Acts 14:1). At Thessalonica Paul's converts were Jews,
many devout Greeks and some leading women (Acts 17:4). In this
and similar instances the social context forced the problem of
race to be an aspect of evangelism. The relation of Jews and

Gentiles in Christ was not only a result of evangelism, but was
an issue, hence a factor, in the process itself. The very
decision to proclaim Christ in a particular social context may
be a form of social action. Such was the case when Peter went
to the house of Cornelius. In antebellum America there were
instances where evangelizing slaves, if accompanied by efforts
to teach them to read the Bible, ran afoul of the law and produced
social conflict. Some states as an effort to forestall slave
uprisings had enacted laws prohibiting teaching them to read.

Evangelism might involve a confrontation with certain customs
and moral practices of a people, not only as a result of evangelism but as interaction with the message itself. At Ephesus Paul's
proclamation of Christ challenged a culture that gave prominence
to idolatry associated with a fertility cult; a riot resulted.
At Thessalonica becoming disciples of Jesus meant turning to God
from idols (I Thessalonians 1:9) and resulted in the evangelists
being charged with turning the world upside down and with acting
against Caesar's decrees (Acts 17:6,7). The very content of the
Gospel and the new relationship to Christ as his disciples was
action that affected social structures. Paul did not see
missions as social or political action. His aim in evangelism
was to "get folks into the Kingdom and then get the Kingdom into
folks" as Dr. Bader used to say. But this process took place in
a social context and interacted with it in such a way as to have
an effect upon it. It was social action.

2. Evangelism is proclaiming Christ or, in Peter's words on
Pentecost, declaring that Jesus is Lord and Christ (Acts 2:38).
Because of the content of this message the process of proclaiming
it is action relating to man's life in the world. When we say
this, we are not forgetting the vertical dimension of the Gospel;
it is the word of salvation. Our concern is to show its social
impact.

In the first place, the proclamation "Jesus is Lord" means
that he has a claim upon the world. To be sure, the proclamation
itself does not define every implication of the Lordship of
Christ for man's life in the world. But to accept that proclamation, to become his disciple, is to acknowledge that every
condition of one's earthly life must be fashioned in obedience to
his authority. All the believer's relationships--to those out-
side the community of faith as well as to those within--must come
to bear the mark of his new identity. Evangelism, which calls
for this decision is action directed toward man's life in the
world. It is social action.

At this point we must digress long enough to deal with the
question of what factors enter into conversion. We cannot insist
that as part of his conversion the believer incorporate particular

ethical attitudes. There are some who do this--making the adop-
tion of a particular ethical stance an aspect of conversion.
Colin Williams articulates such a view:

> . . . for us to ask men to be disciples of Christ without
> enabling them to see how Christ is at work in the race
> revolution, and for us to call men to conversion without
> enabling them to see how Christ calls us all to repent of
> our prejudices and to be open to the fulness of life in
> which there is no black or white, is to practice an evan-
> gelism that can be in fact false witness. . . .
>
> What we are called to today then is an evangelism in
> which calls for decisions for Christ . . . are related to
> calls for decisions "in Christ": to a call to be free for
> the presence with Christ within the struggles of our time
> where Christ is working to overcome prejudice and poverty
> and political irresponsibility and international tribalism
> in order that all men may grow up together as one new man
> in Christ.(19)

In fairness to Williams, he is not substituting ethical decision
for decision to accept Christ. Nevertheless, some serious
questions arise from his joining of the two. Is it not within
one's relationship to Christ that he learns what values are
implied by his conversion? Is it not from that relationship that
he finds the motivation for expressing those values? Where is
the cut-off point, short of complete understanding, for what
values are to be adopted as part of conversion? How does one
avoid the legalism of which missionaries were once guilty when
they made the abandonment of polygamy a part of the conversion
process.(20)

One may be grateful that evangelists in the early church were
unaware of this strategy of making ethical decision part of
conversion. Donald McGavran writes:

> . . . if on the day of Pentecost, Peter had insisted that
> all believers, before they could be baptized into the
> koinonia, had to be willing to practice radical brother-
> hood--eat with pig-eaters and give daughters in marriage
> to uncircumcised believers--he would have killed the
> Church. Fortunately the Holy Spirit led him to keep the
> Church almost entirely Jewish for many years.(21)

We recall a conversation with a frustrated black leader whose
mission board would not allow him to establish any but integrated
congregations. Despite the idealism behind the proscription its
net result was that he could not form a new congregation in the
Watts area of Los Angeles.

It is unfortunate indeed that evangelism in practice has often failed to prepare converts for growth in obedience as disciples and that churches have not edified their members in obedience to the ethical implications of faith. The solution, however, does not consist in making those ethical decisions an essential part of the initial commitment to Christ.

This clarification of the nature of conversion does not mean, however, that persuading men to become Christ's disciples is not social action. By our definition evangelism is social action if it motivates and guides the subsequent life of the believer in the world. Whether the changes it brings about are immediate or only appear after years of discipleship, if these changes come as a consequence of evangelism then evangelism has become an instrument of change in the conditions of earthly life.

The call to discipleship is a call to bring one's whole life under Christ's authority. St. Paul's conversion is an example. "This encounter with Christ," says Michael Green,

> touched Paul at every level of his being. *His mind* was informed and illuminated. . . . *His conscience* was reached. . . . *His emotions* were stirred. . . . But this was a mere incidental on the way to his will, Christ's real goal. *His will* was bent in trusting surrender to Jesus who had called him, and who was from henceforth to be Lord of his life. And in consequence *his life* was transformed: in direction, immediately, and in achievement as time went on.(22)

The fact that Christ calls for the believer to "present" his body gives force to the implication of evangelism for life in the world; for this is the means, as Ernst Käsemann reminds us, by which God takes possession of the world. "What he wants is the world, and that is only possible if he wants our bodies. We are denying him the world whenever we think that we have to give him less or more than our bodies."(23)

There is yet another implication of the Good News for man's life in society, namely, in its affirmation of individual worth. One of the most serious problems of secular culture is that it lacks adequate grounds for affirming the worth of man. In what he calls the "predicament of every human being" in our modern world, Paul Ramsey describes the peril to man's evaluation of himself and others that results from the denial of God.

> When we live by and live out the thought that "God is dead," our own self-understanding and our estimate of the being of others suffer radical alteration. . . . We may think we still place high value upon human life, but the

convictions on which this rests have already been abandoned.
If we still have the *feeling* that man is a thing of worth,
that is only because the checks we draw daily have not yet
cleared the bank, where it will be discovered that the
account is exhausted, indeed . . . *underdeposited.*(24)

The question is, can there be a viable conception of meaningful
social relationships if we cannot confidently assert the worth of
those who participate in those relationships? This was the
problem of a college youth who blurted out his frustration at the
contradiction between what he was being taught about himself in
the classroom and what was expected of him in society.

If men are but animals why not treat them as such? If man
is a slave to determinism. . . . what is the value of the
ballot, trial by jury and civil liberties in general? . . .
Personally I fail to understand how you can expect us to
be ardent Christians and democrats when the vital postu-
lates on which these faiths are supposed to rest are daily
undermined in the classroom.(25)

Our point is that the Gospel has implications for our view of
man and his worth, implications which affect man in his understanding of himself and others with whom he transacts. The
Gospel declares: He dies for our sins. The Cross is therefore
a verdict of man's worth.(26) The resurrection of Jesus is likewise as assertion of man's worth. His resurrection is the pledge
of our own resurrection; it witnesses to the intention of God for
the persons he created for fellowship and therefore declares
their value in his sight. This truth is vividly brought out in
Ramsey's analysis of Dostoevski's concept that without the idea
of immortality any treatment of one's neighbor is permissible.
It is not merely the threat of punishment, but what one feels
about the significance of human life that is the basis for
morality in human relationships.

Without immortality, which in sum contains all God's
estimate of human life, anything is permitted which the
necessity of the historical situation seems to require
of us for the good of the group or cause to which we
belong.(27)

The Gospel is a disclosure of the value of persons in the eyes of
God; one can relate to all human beings on the basis of this
assertion of their worth. Preaching this Gospel is social action.

3. We must also consider whether the church's role in evangelism is a type of social action. The church has the mission of
evangelizing the world. As an aspect of this commission its very
nature as a structured community should have an impact upon the

society around it. The church is the body of Christ which means,
says Ernst Käsemann, that the church is the "present sphere" of
Christ's sovereignty, "in which he deals with the world through
Word, sacrament and the sending forth of Christians, and in which
he finds obedience even before his parousia."(28)

A similar implication derives from the fact the church is the
people of God--a holy nation comprised of persons out of all
nations of the earth. Along with its mandate to proclaim Christ
the church has the vocation of exhibiting the Gospel in both
content and effect. When it is faithful to its vocation as a
holy nation, the church exhibits in its own life the possibility
of the uniting of all humanity in Christ. If it is objected that
this is an accompaniment of evangelism and not evangelism itself
we respond: if the accompaniment of evangelism touches man's
life in society evangelism should be given credit for the change.

There is, however, a more direct result of the church's involvement in evangelism. The church is that society to which persons
are added when they become Christ's disciples. The church is the
locus of that interaction with the social context that occurs when
the Gospel is preached. When the church--existing as a particular,
identifiable society within a culture--as an aspect of evangelism
receives into its fellowship the despised, the weak, the foolish,
the slave, the man of another race, along with the noble, the
strong, the wise, the free, and the native born, it confronts
that culture with a new norm of obedience to God, a new norm of
what it means to be human. It raises an issue for that culture
as to its own values. This is social action, and it is hardly a
by-product of evangelism because it occurs at the moment someone
heeds the call to discipleship. Paul reminds the Colossians,
"Onesimus [the slave] is one of you." (Colossians 4:9) He tells
Philemon to receive Onesimus as a brother and as a partner
(Philemon 16,17). In these instances at least the social implications of evangelism are immediate. We scarcely need to mention
the tragic results that occur when the church incorporates into
its own life the barriers erected by the world rather than over-
coming those barriers in obedience to the Gospel.(29)

There is a final consideration that has to do with the meaning
of Matthew 25:31-46, the picture of judgment that concludes
Christ's eschatalogical discourse. This text is invoked more
than any other in support of social action as the proper focus
of mission. "Inasmuch as ye have done it unto one of the least
of these my brethren, ye have done it unto me."

Is this text a counter-argument for evangelism as the primary
mission? Does it lay a foundation for social involvement
separate from the good news that "God was in Christ, reconciling
the world unto himself?" We believe not. Rather, we believe

that the reference to the Son of man found here--if taken in context--combines with other Son of man references in Matthew's Gospel to provide the historical and eschatological dimensions for the Christian's understanding of his life and action in the world.

At the end of history stands the Son of man before whom all appear in judgment. But he is also the Son of man who appeared in history to bear the judgment in behalf of all men (Isaiah 53). He is the suffering servant, the Son of man who "came not to be ministered unto, but to minister and to give his life a ransom for many" (Matthew 20:28). In this act of ministry he identified himself with mankind; they are his brothers. In all things "it behooved him to be made like unto his brethren" (Hebrews 2:11,17). Hence he recognizes ministry done to his brethren as done to himself.

The surprise of the sheep is not in the discovery that they are disciples. They know who their Lord is. Their surprise is in his estimate "ye have done it unto me." Imbued with his spirit of ministry in which he placed value on persons and declared that value on the cross, these people had themselves invested worth in mankind for which he had given his life. For them to have served others to "gain points" with the Lord would have been crass legalism--achieving acceptability by their deeds. No wonder they are surprised. They had become his disciples; to be a disciple is to await the hope of his coming through faithful stewardship, which is the message of the whole of chapter 25 of Matthew. For them discipleship meant the acceptance of his verdict of human worth and the giving of themselves in compassionate service expressive of that verdict. Their relationship to their Lord had changed their relationships with each other.

In what we have been asserting the presumption has been that if in evangelism the ground is laid for changes in the conditions of man's earthly life, evangelism is social action. This is not to make such changes in themselves the goal of mission, or to minimize other acts of social involvement undertaken by Christians within the structures of their life--job, community, nation. The people of God can be faithful to the mandate to proclaim Christ and persuade men to become his disciples and responsible members of his church in the confidence that in this function they are partners with God in turning the world right side up.

NOTES

1. Jesse Bader, "The Divine Impetuosity," *Christian Evangelist*,
   LXI, 8 (February 21, 1924), p. 243.

2. "He that Winneth Souls is Wise," Christian Standard, LV, 44
   (July 31, 1920), p. 1.

3. Arthur F. Glasser, Unpublished lecture, Fuller Theological
   Seminary, 1973.

4. Langdon Gilkey, *How the Church Can Minister to the World
   Without Losing Itself* (New York, 1964), pp. 63-64. Reprinted
   by permission of Harper and Row.

5. Newbigen, *Honest Religion for Secular Man*, pp. 147-148.
   Reprinted by permission of Westminster Press.

6. Brevard S. Childs, *Biblical Theology in Crisis* (Philadelphia,
   1970), p. 125. Reprinted by permission of Westminster Press.
   Cf. Forell, *Proclamation of the Gospel*, pp. 109-110.

7. See the discussion of Jürgen Moltmann, "Political Theology,"
   Theology Today, XXVIII, 2 (April, 1971), pp. 6-23.

8. Suzanne De Dietrich, *Witnessing Community* (Philadelphia,
   1958), pp. 16-17. Reprinted by permission of Westminster
   Press.

9. Gilkey sees this as a pervasive tendency in evangelical
   thought until recently. *How the Church Can Minister*, pp. 32-
   33. See also David O. Moberg's analysis, "Barriers to
   Effective Social Concern," in his *Great Reversal* (New York,
   1972), pp. 86-103. The 1974 Lausanne Covenant (Theme 6), on
   the other hand, strongly advocates participation in the world
   by Christians.

10. Moberg, *op. cit.*, pp. 87-89.

11. Gilkey, *How the Church Can Minister*, pp. 48-49. The term
    "culture-Protestantism" is used by H. Richard Neibuhr,
    Christ and Culture (New York, 1951), Ch. 3.

12. John C. Bennett, "The Church and the Secular," *Christianity
    and Crisis*, XXV, 22 (December 26, 1966), p. 296. Cf. the
    analysis of Donald A. McGavran, "A Criticism of the WCC
    Working Draft on Mission," in McGavran, ed., *Eye of the Storm*,
    pp. 233-241.

13. Childs, *op. cit.*, p. 101.

14. See Cynthia Wedel, "Where the People Are," *Theology Today*,
    XXXII, 1 (April, 1973), pp. 44-45. John Mulder, "Who Speaks
    To the Church," *Theology Today*, XXX, 2 (July, 1973), pp. 163-
    164.

15. See the statement by Dean E. Walker on the role of the congregation in communicating Christ's authority in mission, service, and vocation, "Authority," *Christian Educators Journal*, III, 2 (Summer, 1971), pp. 6-7.

16. Andrew M. Greeley, "Politics and Political Theologians," *Theology Today*, XXX, 4 (January, 1974), pp. 390-391. Reprinted by permission of the author and *Theology Today*. See also Gilkey, *How the Church Can Minister*, pp. 71-73. Forell, *op. cit.*, pp. 109-114. Moberg, *op. cit.*, p. 51.

17. Moberg reaches a similar conclusion in his study of Evangelical social concern, *The Great Reversal*, pp. 177 ff.

18. See Donald A. McGavran's description of this crisis, "Two Theologies of Mission Battle for Control," *The Church Herald*, Vol. 98, No. 11 (November 28, 1975), pp. 10-12.

19. Williams, *Faith in a Secular Age*, pp. 116-118. Reprinted by permission of Harper and Row.

20. See Newbigen, *op. cit.*, pp. 73-74.

21. Donald A. McGavran, "Essential Evangelism . . . ," McGavran, ed., *Eye of the Storm*, p. 60. Reprinted by permission of Donald A. McGavran.

22. Michael Green, Evangelism in the Early Church, p. 161. Reprinted by permission of Eerdmans.

23. Käsemann, *Perspectives on Paul*, pp. 114-115. Reprinted by permission of Fortress Press.

24. Paul Ramsey, *Nine Modern Moralists*, (C) 1962, p. 19. Reprinted by permission of Prentice-Hall, Inc., Englewood Cliffs, N.J.

25. Henry P. Van Dusen, *God in Education* (New York, 1951), pp. 54-55. Reprinted by permission of Charles Scribner's Sons.

26. Moltmann takes up the theme of the suffering of God as loving identification with mankind in *The Crucified God* (New York, 1974), p. 244.

27. Ramsey, *op. cit.*, p. 21. Reprinted by permission of Prentice-Hall, Inc., Englewood Cliffs, N.J.

28. Käsemann, *op. cit.*, p. 117. Reprinted by permission of Fortress Press.

29. Forell, *op. cit.*, 103, discusses the ambiguity of the church's behavior in opposing changes its own message has helped to produce.

4

Renewal
Is for Mission

"The salvation of a church that has almost lost its Lord lies not
in forgetting him, but in finding him again in its life."(1)   So
wrote Langdon Gilkey a decade ago as the effects of the secularization of theology were already being experienced in the churches.
The assertion that the church needs renewal scarcely requires
defense.   A crisis of faith exists in many quarters.   The pulpit
is often an uncertain trumpet.   The sense of being gripped by a
dynamic faith is lost to many members of the church, thereby
denying to them the means for motivating and guiding their life
in the day to day world where they carry out their responsibilities.   Despite the optimistic hope a generation ago of Christian
unity as the great fact of our time, there is more splintering of
the household of faith than before.   There is uncertainty about
the nature of the church's task and whether missions should be
undertaken at all.   Also evident is the gap between the church's
profession and its performance; "the acts of your koinonia speak
so loudly that we cannot hear the words of your kerygma."(2)
Churches have declined in membership and attendance.   Unhappily
the response to this decline has often been inward: how to recoup
the losses, how to strengthen the institution.   Evangelism has
often been undertaken for unworthy reasons: to regain the lapsed,
to gain needed members for support of programs.   Church programs--
even worship--have become "client-oriented," aimed more at
retaining members than training them for service in the Kingdom
of God.

Although the situation today gives urgency to the appeal for
renewal, the idea itself is not new.   Throughout their history the

people of God are constantly confronted by the image of their true identity as given in the covenant and challenged to renew their life as a community, and as individuals, by the terms of that covenant. Implicit to this renewal--the reformation of the church's life in terms of the understanding of itself given in the covenant--is the recovery of the vocation given to the people of God. The self-understanding of the community and its sense of vocation are inseparable. Hence, while renewal has to do with the quality of life of the people of God it necessarily includes the recovery of their vocation.(3)

Renewal, as W. A. Visser 'T Hooft reminds us, is not mere innovation, "the creation of something different for the sake of change or for the sake of adaptation to the most recent historical developments."(4) Moreover, since the church stands under the grace of God as well as under his judgment, the appeal for renewal does not mean rejecting the church as it has existed since the first century. It is as wrong to write "Void" over the history of the church because of its failures as it is wrong to accept as valid or normative every development that has appeared in its life in history.

The concern of this chapter is the basis and goal of the renewal of the church. To keep the treatment as brief as possible we are focusing attention primarily on the seventeenth chapter of the Fourth Gospel. Here is recorded Jesus' high priestly prayer on the night of his betrayal and arrest. The prayer focuses upon the purpose of the Father. Jesus' concern is the relation of his own mission and, in turn, the mission of the apostles and of the church to the Father's purpose. We may summarize these relationships as follows:

(1) In Jesus' understanding God's purpose is fellowship; ". . . this is life eternal, that they might know thee the only true God, and Jesus Christ, whom thou hast sent."(v. 3). Knowing God in the Biblical sense is primarily personal; it is fellowship with him.

(2) God is acting to create fellowship through revelation of his glory in Jesus. Jesus identifies his own mission as making the Father's name known to the apostles and through them to the world (vv. 24-25). The apostles' mission stands in relation to that of Jesus. They have been "given" to him (v. 6) and believe the Father sent him (v. 8). They have been given his word (vv. 7, 14). As the Father sent Jesus into the world so now Jesus is sending the apostles into the world (v. 18). Through their word men may come to faith in Jesus and so become his disciples (v. 20).

(3) Jesus also envisions the creation of a community made up of those who believe in him through the word of the apostles.

This community has the vocation of making known to the world the
intention of God and its fulfillment in Christ. He prays that
those who believe in him may be one in order "that the world may
believe that thou hast sent me" (v. 21). This prayer of Jesus
assumes the mission of the church.

This correlation of the role of the church and the purpose of
God is not artificial, nor is it unique to the New Testament. It
aptly describes the relation of Israel's mission to God's self-
disclosure in the Exodus. In the Old Testament tradition this
event is viewed as being at once a revelatory, elective, redemp-
tive act of God which brought Israel into being as a servant
community.

Jesus' prayer for his people, who believe in him through the
apostles' word, describes them in terms that serve as a model for
the continual reformation of their life: (1) Through their faith
in him they are brought into community. (2) This community finds
its understanding of itself in its relation to the Father and the
Son. (3) The unity resulting from this relationship of disciples
to Jesus is one of the marks of the community's existence. (4)
The community exists for mission--"that the world may believe."
Renewal then is the recovery of the identity and the unity of the
people of God that derives from their relation to the Lord, so
they may fulfill their task in the world.

CHRISTIAN UNITY IS FOR MISSION

In the prayer of Jesus the mission of the church is indispens-
ably related to his own mission and that of the apostles. Just as
Jesus' mission is bound up with his identity with the Father so
the mission of the church is bound up with its identity in Christ.
The theme of election, for example, which many have avoided
because of its mistaken identification with predestination, is
tied to the theme of mission. God elects the covenant community
for the purpose of mission. They are set apart from the world in
order to be sent into the world.(5)

The conception of mission belongs to both Old and New Testa-
ments. Israel was elected and redeemed to be the people of God;
as God's people Israel's vocation was to serve him. Out of
loyalty to him who called her, Israel must mold her life in
obedience to the covenant and give her life in his service.(6)
Israel's mission consisted in the fact that as a people for God's
own possession she existed among other peoples as a kingdom of
priests. As a nation Israel was to perform a priestly ministry
to other nations (Exodus 19:5, 6).(7) Israel's mission was implied,
moreover, in the fact she worshipped the one God. If there is but
one God, he is the God of all nations, even though it was Israel

who now was called to his worship. It was Israel's task to
exhibit his glory to all the nations.(8)

The theme of election to mission is taken up also in the New
Testament. The church is an elect community--redeemed in fellowship with God in Christ. But she bears this mark of identity and
must be faithful to it so that she may be his instrument for
evangelizing the world. Peter reminds his readers that they are
"a chosen [elect] generation, a royal priesthood, a holy nation,
a peculiar people"--a description reminiscent of Exodus 19:5, 6.
You are these things, he says, "that he should shew forth the
praises of him who hath called you out of darkness into his
marvelous light" (I Peter 2:9).

Although both are elected to mission there is a difference
between the New and the Old Israel. Johannes Blauw in his
monumental study, *The Missionary Nature of the Church*, describes
this difference in terms of the relation of the two communities
to the salvation brought to mankind in Christ. The Old Testament
Israel "in anticipation" represented "the salvation of the world."
The Church, on the other hand, "represents the salvation that has
come in Christ." Hence there is a dimension in the mission of
the Church which was not present to the mission of the Old Testament Israel, namely, "acts of proclamation in behalf of Christ."
(9)

Why then in the prayer of Jesus does he link the unity of his
people to their vocation of bringing the world to confess his
name? Many answers have been suggested. Some appeal to the
practical, to the need for efficiency or economy in getting the
job done. Others invoke cultural factors; our age is the age of
the great corporation--in government, in business, in agriculture,
and so on. The church will relate to such a culture by being
itself a corporation. One detects in some movements for unity
today a spirit of retrenchment and consolidation.

Unity is related to mission because of the nature of the
church as the Body of Christ. No figure of the church so vividly
identifies the church with the intention and mission of Jesus.
In an analysis of this theme in St. Paul, Ernest Käsemann writes:
"The exalted Christ really has an earthly body, and believers
with their whole being are actually incorporated into it and have
therefore to behave accordingly."(10) As the Body of Christ the
church "is the means whereby Christ reveals himself on earth and
becomes incarnate in the world through his Spirit."(11) H. H.
Rowley in his well-known study of the Biblical meaning of election
agrees; the church, he declares, is "an extension of the personality of Christ, infused with His Spirit and the organ of His
activity in the world."(12)

While preaching Christ is its primary task, the church's vocation extends beyond the proclamation of the Gospel. It has the
task also of embodying that revelation in its life. It is to
exhibit in its very life both the content and the effect of the
Gospel--in reconciliation and in service. Here is the reason
behind Christ's passion for the unity of his people. Division
weakens the capacity of the church to exhibit by its life the good
news of God's reconciling love in Jesus Christ.

Unity is not an end in itself but a means for carrying out the
mission. The same must also be said for the concept of restoration, by which we mean the appeal to the New Testament as the
basis of renewal. Restoration is not a goal in itself but a means
to the goal of world evangelism. This is so for two reasons. On
the one hand, since the church has its origin in the disclosure of
God in Christ, it must bear in its life the marks of its origin.
It is, in the words of the hymn writer, "the heaven drawn picture
of Christ the living word." Nothing can be of permanent or normative significance for the church that does not bear the marks of
its relationship to the living Lord. At the same time, if the
church was created for mission it must embody in itself what it is
seeking to accomplish. If the church's task is to bring persons
to a saving knowledge of God in Christ and to help them grow in
that relationship (to become responsible members of his body) the
church itself must possess the corresponding marks: (1) of faith
in Christ, (2) the sacraments as divinely given institutions of
the Gospel, and (3) ministries of teaching and oversight for edify-
ing believers in the responsibilities of the new life, Whether
considered from the standpoint of the Gospel from which they
derive or from the standpoint of the goal toward which they are
directed, which is presenting "every man perfect in Christ Jesus"
(Colossians 1:28), the identifying marks of the church are the
same. The faith, the sacraments, the teaching all have their
focus in the person of Christ, who is the Lord whom the Christian
confesses, the mediator who brings him into fellowship with God,
and the model for an obedient life in this world. So with equal
force one may say: "The Gospel is the criterion for the church"
and "The mission is the criterion for the church."

Mission is the goal both of restoration and unity. Does this
mean that efforts in evangelism should be suspended until the
church has been brought to unity and renewal? Must reformation
precede mission?(13) Does the failure of the church to exhibit
the marks of the Gospel in every aspect of its life mean it can
no longer be the instrument of his mission?(14)

There are, to be sure, elements of paradox in the answer to
these questions. To suggest that reformation must precede efforts
to evangelize runs in the face of the uniform witness of the New
Testament. No hint is to be found there that the carrying out of

the mission of the church must await the church's growth to
maturity, however desirable the latter may be. Moreover, it
overlooks the meaning of Christ's message, in which the word of
grace accompanies his word of judgment. Peter's sermon on
Pentecost is a case in point. The convicting word and the word
of forgiveness came together: "God hath made that same Jesus,
whom ye have crucified, both Lord and Christ. . . . Repent, and
be baptized . . . in the name of Jesus for the remission of sins,
and ye shall receive the gift of the Holy Spirit" (Acts 2:36, 38).
Applied to his people the grace and truth of the Lord means that
he accepts them even while calling them to repentance. The prayer
of Jesus for his apostles (John 17) appears in the context of the
last week where the weaknesses of their discipleship are exposed;
despite this, he commits his mission to them.

However, the fact of God's grace does not nullify the appeal
for renewal for the sake of mission. Nowhere does the message
of Jesus use the fact of God's acceptance of us in spite of our
sinfulness to eliminate the call for continuing reformation of
life. It is so with his treatment of the church. Like the
apostle it is an earthen vessel (II Corinthians 4:7). But it
bears a divine treasure and, like the apostle, must endeavor to
be a vessel fit for the Master's use.

UNITY IS "IN CHRIST"

To return to our analysis of John 17, in his prayer Jesus
indicates the kind of unity he wills for his people. It is a
unity that is personal in nature; he likens it to the oneness of
his relation to the Father: "That they may be one, as thou,
Father, art in me, and I in thee, that they also may be one in
us" (v. 21). Believers experience unity among themselves by
virtue of being in relationship to Jesus and the Father. Hence,
their unity derives from that relationship.

Viewed from this perspective it seems that we have often made
the unity of believers more complicated than did the Lord himself.
The complication is partly due, of course, to the factors of
history we inherit, which color our perceptions and restrict our
vision of the possibilities for obedience to our Lord.

We can gain much insight into the meaning of Christian unity
from an examination of the unity of the apostolic community
gathered about Jesus in the Upper Room. They are the church in
embryo--the *ecclesia designata*.(15) Their unity, consisting in
their mutual relation to Christ (v. 11), is a model for our own.

The unity of the apostolic community was Jesus' gift to them
and not their own achievement. Apart from him there were few

ways these men could have participated together in anything. Even
in the context of their Jewishness they had differences that
would have kept them apart. They differed in economic status,
in social status, in learning. They differed in piety; one of
their number had been a tax collector, who in the popular mind
was usually grouped with harlots. There must have been many
differences of temperament, habits of life, and outlook on the
world that would have prevented their being drawn together on
human terms. Their unity could only come as a gift vouchsafed to
them in his invitation to discipleship.

The unity of the apostles was not institutional or structural
in our usual sense of the term. One can, of course, refer to
their relation to him as a type of structure, just as the relation of parents to children, and of children to each other are
structures. The apostles were related to him as believers, as
disciples, as servants accepting his call to mission. In this
relationship lay their unity. But they did not themselves
create structures in order to have unity; nor would any structures they might create to express their unity have been essential
to it. Their unity consisted in their relation to Jesus. Commitment to him and to the commission continued thereafter to be the
bond that held them together. In this respect they are an example
to the church. It is the bond his people have with Christ that
creates and defines their relation to each other.

This attitude toward the oneness of the church was clearly
articulated at Montreal in 1963.

> In our discussion of the relation of the churches to the
> Church we have found it helpful to think not in terms of
> the churches as parts of the one Church, but rather of
> the Church as the Body of Christ, including the saints of
> all ages and the Christians of all places, which is both
> present and one with the local congregation gathered for
> the hearing of the Word and the celebration of the Lord's
> Supper according to Christ's ordinance. "Wherever Jesus
> Christ is there is the Catholic Church." *Thus each church
> or congregation participating in Christ is related to
> others not by participation in some higher structure but
> rather by an identity of existence in Christ* [Italics
> mine].(16)

Again, the unity of the apostles did not consist in their
achievement of a given level of understanding of Jesus' teaching.
The Gospels reflect how slow they were to grasp the meaning of
his words and how much they differed in what they understood. It
was not doctrinal concensus that bound them together; it was the
oneness of their commitment to him. This truth may be clearer to
us as we realize that believers are like children in a family,

whose unity lies not in their level of intellectual attainment
but in their mutual relation to their parents. This realization
lay at the basis of Thomas Campbell's objections to creedal
statements as bonds of unity. It was not that the doctrines they
stated were necessarily untrue. It was their inherent presumption
that Christians can possess the same level of understanding of the
truth, whereas, he said, "There have always been young men as well
as old men in the faith."(17)

The New Testament does not make a virtue of ignorance. Being
his disciple implies both the desire and the endeavor to learn of
him. The neglect of such learning means the impoverishment of
one's vision of the possibilities and responsibilities of his new
humanity. Nevertheless, even those who faithfully seek understanding will not reach the same level of it. They are not
thereby divided from each other. Unity of believers consists in
their relation to him; it is personal.

Again, the oneness of the apostolic community did not consist
in their level of spiritual attainment. They were not always
Christlike. They were not always humble; John would have for-
bidden anyone not of their number to cast out demons in the name
of Jesus. Some sought honor above the rest. One had an
impetuous tongue. Another doubted. Without repentance, any of
these faults could have led to breach of faith and thus to breach
of unity. As long as a relation of love and trust existed between
the believer and the Lord no failure experienced in the course of
growth could break the bond of fellowship. In this relation they
found the basis for their fellowship with each other. The family
of God--like the families of men--will always have in it the young
as well as the mature. Their oneness lies in their commitment to
the purposes of the family and not in their approximate successes
in realizing this goal.

The unity of the apostles, while his gift and not their achievement, still depended upon their obedient faith for its realization.
In his prayer for them Jesus recognizes that the apostles "have
known . . . that I came out from thee, and . . . have believed
that thou didst send me (v. 8). Alan Richardson, in his study of
the meaning of the terms *know* and *believe* in John's gospel,
declares that the two words "if they are not synonymous, are fully
complementary. Believing (hearing and obeying) results in knowing
(personally experiencing), and one cannot know if one will not
believe." Hence, he concludes: "To know that Christ comes from
God is possible only to those who know Christ personally in the
subjective relation of loving trust and obedience."(18)

The unity of Christ's body, of which the apostles' unity is
the model, is a oneness in Christ. It is his gift received through
obedient faith.

THE NORM FOR UNITY AND RENEWAL - THE APOSTLES' WORD

There remains for our consideration the matter of how his
people may realize the unity Christ wills for them. In his
priestly prayer Jesus ascribes this role to his apostles who are
to be ministers of the new covenant. Throughout the passage
Jesus identifies the mission of the apostles with his own mission.
As he has been sent into the world by the Father, so now he is
sending the apostles into the world. He will give them the
Spirit who shall, in his words, "take of mine and . . . shew it
unto you" (John 16:7-15).

The relation between their ministry and the unity of the
church may be stated as follows: (1) The relation of believers
to each other has its basis in their relation to Christ, a
relation of loving trust and obedience. (2) The word of the
apostles communicates this faith. Those for whose unity Jesus
prays are those who will be brought to faith in him through the
word of the apostles (v. 20). (3) The apostles' word--as the
word that calls men to faith--is then the norm of that faith and
the relationship built upon it.

The apostles are the ministers of the new covenant (II
Corinthians 3:6). By their word they identify the Lord, guide
men in their submission to his authority, and teach them his
will for their lives. These functions are illustrated by their
role as described by Luke on the first Pentecost when the new
law was given (acts 2). The Holy Spirit, in accordance with
Jesus' promise, came upon the apostles (vv. 1-13). As their
spokesman Peter proclaimed the inauguration of the new kingdom
over which Jesus rules as Lord (vv. 14-36). He offered forgiveness of sin and the gift of the Holy Spirit through obedient
faith (vv. 36-40). The new community thus brought into being
"continued steadfastly in the apostles' doctrine and fellowship,
and in breaking of bread, and in prayers" (vv. 41-47).

The people of God then are a covenant community. Elected
and redeemed by God's grace they have fellowship with him whom
to know is life eternal. They are in pilgrimage, journeying
toward their Canaan of eschatological promise, and seeking to be
f thful to the vocation given them by their Lord. The Word of
the apostles, which is the word of the new covenant, becomes the
permanent point of reference for their life, the norm by which
all developments of their life in history are to be measured.
The Scriptures as they embody the apostolic tradition communicate
this norm to the church in ages subsequent to that of the apostles.
Herein is the significance of the canon, in the view of Brevard
Childs; the canon identifies authority for the church. The
Scriptures contain not only examples of the obedient life, but

the norm of the obedient life. "The Scriptures of the church,"
says Childs, "provide the authoritative and definitive word that
continues to shape and enliven the church."(19)

Some, however, have objected that the church does not find its
norm so much by reference to the past as by reference to the
future--to the Christian hope. The appeal to the past is
associated in their minds with a static definition of the church,
whereas what is needed is a more dynamic conception, based upon
an "orientation toward the future."(20) Such a view is expressed
by Colin Williams. While we should be loyal to the emphasis upon
the "'given' form of the church coming to us out of the past,"
nevertheless he declared, "loyalty to the 'past' Christ is main-
tained only by being open to him as he comes to us out of the
future."(21)

There is no question that the element of hope figures promi-
nently in the church's self-understanding. The people of God in
pilgrimage see themselves not only as having come from somewhere
but also as going somewhere, and that somewhere is an important
element in their life. This is vividly illustrated in Israel's
movement from Egypt to Canaan. God had adopted Israel; the
nation was his heir. Therefore the people saw their life from
the perspective of both elective grace and of fulfillment. No
doubt their goal served as a measure of their progress. It
motivated their obedience as they met the challenges posed by new
situations they encountered along the way. But the clue to their
understanding of their nature as a community lay in the covenant,
and it was the self-understanding derived from the covenant that
gave shape to their obedience in whatever circumstances they
found themselves. Such was the view of the prophets. Even after
the people settled in the land and their hope took on new forms
of anticipation of the future, the prophets still called upon
Israel to be faithful to the election tradition. Israel's sin,
in their view, was a betrayal of her own past, her existence as
God's covenant people. The way to renewal was by recommitment to
the covenant.(22) It is so with the people of God of the new
covenant. They, too, are motivated by their hope of the consummation of God's elective grace. Through their faithfulness to him
in obedience they will be brought into their inheritance. However,
their understanding of their character as a community and the
obedience that flows from that understanding both derive from the
covenant given in the apostolic word.

Another problem related to the above discussion of norm has to
do with the validity of the concept of restoration. In the minds
of some restoration is identified with a static conception of the
church in which, without differentiation, all the elements of the
life of the first-century church are taken as normative for the

church today. Perhaps it is this view of restoration that has led
some to say it is untenable and divisive. It seems that the
detractors of restoration along with many of its advocated con-
ceive of it in the same way. If applied to Israel it would have
required the people to go back to their beginning, to reassemble
at the base of Mt. Sinai where the covenant was given and the
nation constituted. Applied to the church it would mean a return
to the conditions of the church's life at Jerusalem in 30 A.D. or
at Corinth in 55 A.D.

The church was not produced by the written New Testament but
by the new covenant itself, given by the apostles and now incorporated in the Scriptures. Restoration is the appeal to that
covenant as the norm for the church's life. The church needs
such a norm lest it commit the idolatry of sancitfying every
development in its historical life as the will of God.

This writer recalls an address given three decades ago by the
venerable Frederick D. Kershner, dean emeritus of the School of
Religion, Butler University. He had been asked by the students
to speak to the question: Shall we throw the plea overboard?
His response, to which he devoted considerable time, was: "If we
throw it overboard there will surely be many who will jump in to
retrieve it." The dean's prophecy proved correct. It is encourag-
ing to hear other voices like that of W. A. Visser 'T Hooft, one-
time president of the World Council of Churches, advocating
renewal in these terms:

> Every true renewal of the Church is based on the hearing
> anew of the Word of God as it comes to us in the Bible. . . .
> There have . . . been many who have sought the renewal of
> the Church by breaking away from the Bible or by adding to
> and improving upon the Bible. But we must maintain this
> simple truth that outside the Word of God there is in the
> world no true source of renewal. Why is that so? Because
> the Bible is the authentic record of the only radically new
> event that has ever taken place in the world. . . . It
> [the Church] can only break out of the old world by submitting
> itself to the judgment and inspiration of God's revelation
> itself and that revelation is given to us through the Holy
> Scriptures. Here alone a true dialogue can take place
> between the Church and its Lord. Here the Church discovers
> that it needs renewal and what renewal means. This "orienta-
> tion to the Centre" (Cullman) has been and is the great life-
> giving force in the Church and this is the true return to
> the source. . . . It is in listening to the Word of God in
> the Scriptures that the Church discovers again and again
> what God's design is and what its own place is in that
> design. (23)

In a similar manner, and from still a different quarter, Fr. Hans
Küng contends that the message of the New Testament is the
"essential norm" for the life of the church in every age. Not
every development in the church's history, says Küng, can be
"authorized by its origins," hence the need of the church to
"orient itself anew" using as its guide "the word of Jesus Christ,
as testified by the apostles."(24) The readiness of this noted
Roman Catholic theologian to use the term *restore*(25) should give
pause to the tendency of many contemporary churchmen to dismiss
the concept of restoration as having no validity for the church
today.

In the shadow of the cross Jesus prayed for the unity of his
people that they might carry out his mandate to evangelize the
world. His people find their unity and renewal through loving
trust and obedience to the risen Lord, which is the meaning of
faith. The word of the apostles as the means of communicating
this faith is the norm for the renewal of the church.

There is probably no time in the church's historical existence
that is not a time of crisis; and so we may describe the times in
which we live. They are particularly critical, however, not only
because the challenge of the world's need is so great, but
because of the uncertainty of so many Christians about the kind
of response they should be making to this challenge. We hear
voices today calling for relevance and other voices calling for
faithfulness. Christians must seek to be both faithful and
relevant. It is our conviction, hopefully reflected above, that
in faithfulness to the Lord and his mandate the church can be
relevant to the needs of the world.

NOTES

1. Gilkey, *How the Church Can Minister*, p. 146.

2. Hoekendijk, "The Call to Evangelism" McGavran, ed., *Eye of
   the Storm*, p. 54.

3. See Hugh Kerr, "The Church and Change," *Theology Today*,
   XXVIII, 1 (April, 1971), pp. 3-4.

4. W. A. Visser 'T Hooft, *Renewal of the Church* (Philadelphia,
   1956), p. 12.

5. Dietrich, *Witnessing Community*, p. 16.

6. See H. H. Rowley, *Biblical Doctrine of Election*, new ed.
   (London, 1964), pp. 46-60.

7. See Johannes Blauw, *Missionary Nature of the Church* (New York, 1962), p. 24, in support of this understanding of Exodus 19:5, 6.

8. Rowley, *op. cit.*, p. 62.

9. Blauw, *op. cit.*, p. 80.

10. Käsemann, *Perspectives on Paul*, p. 104. Reprinted by permission of Fortress Press.

11. *Ibid.*, p. 117.

12. Rowley, *op. cit.*, p. 167.

13. See the rejoinder given by McGavran, "Essential Evangelism . . .," *Eye of the Storm*, pp. 59-60.

14. Described by Porteous, *Search for Christian Credibility*, pp. 184-185. Cf. Shaull, "Does Religion Demand Social Change," *Theology Today*, XXVI, 1 (April, 1969), p. 15.

15. See Ralph E. Knudsen, *Theology of the New Testament* (Chicago, 1964), p. 327.

16. Fourth World Conference on Faith and Order, Montreal, 1963, Section I.

17. *Declaration and Address*, Propositions 7, 8.

18. Alan Richardson, *Introduction to the Theology of the New Testament* (New York, 1958), pp. 45-46. Reprinted by permission of Harper and Row.

19. Brevard S. Childs, *Biblical Theology in Crisis*, pp. 101-105. Cf. Gilkey, *How the Church Can Minister*, p. 77.

20. See George S. Hendry, "Eclipse of Creation," *Theology Today*, XXVIII, 4 (January, 1972), pp. 424-425, for a critique of this approach in theology.

21. Colin Williams, *Faith in a Secular Age*, p. 104.

22. Gerhard von Rad, *Old Testament Theology*, Vol. II, *The Theology of Israel's Prophetic Tradition*, D. M. G. Stalker, trans. (New York, 1965), pp. 176-177. G. Ernest Wright, *God Who Acts* (London, 1952), stresses the "recital" of God's past action as determinative of Israel's worship and obedience.

23. Visser 'T Hooft, *op. cit.*, pp. 91-93. Reprinted by permission of Westminster Press.

24. Hans Küng, *The Church* (New York, 1967), preface p. xi., p. 24.

25. *Ibid.*, p. 414.

William J. Richardson has been on the faculty of Northwest Christian College, Eugene, Oregon, since 1947, teaching in the areas of New Testament and history. He holds degrees from Northwest Christian College (B.Th.), Butler University (B.D., M.A.), and the University of Oregon (Ph.D.). He has been called upon frequently for lectures at college campuses, church conventions, and Air Force Spiritual Life conferences. He has published articles in the *Christian Educator's Journal* and *Interpretation*.

BOOKS BY THE WILLIAM CAREY LIBRARY

GENERAL

The Birth of Missions in America by Charles L. Chaney, $7.95 paper, 352 pp.

Church Growth and Christian Mission by Donald A. McGavran, $4.95x paper, 256 pp.

Committed Communities: Fresh Streams for World Missions by Charles J. Mellis, $3.95 paper, 160 pp.

The Conciliar-Evangelical Debate: The Crucial Documents, 1964-1976 edited by Donald McGavran, $8.95 paper, 400 pp.

Crucial Dimensions in World Evangelization edited by Arthur F. Glasser et al., $6.95x paper, 480 pp.

Evangelical Missions Tomorrow edited by Wade T. Coggins and Edwin L. Frizen, Jr., $5.95 paper, 208 pp.

The Growth Crisis in the American Church: A Presbyterian Case Study by Foster H. Shannon, $4.95 paper, 176 pp.

Here's How: Health Education by Extension by Ronald and Edith Seaton, $3.45 paper, 144 pp.

A Manual for Church Growth Surveys by Ebbie C. Smith, $3.95 paper, 144 pp.

On the Move with the Master: A Daily Devotional Guide on World Mission by Duain W. Vierow, $4.95 paper, 176 pp.

Readings in Third World Missions: A Collection of Essential Documents edited by Marlin L. Nelson, $6.95x paper, 304 pp.

The 25 Unbelievable Years: 1945-1969 by Ralph D. Winter, $2.95 paper, 128 pp.

World Handbook for the World Christian by Patrick St. J. St. G. Johnstone, $4.95 paper, 224 pp.

THEOLOGICAL EDUCATION BY EXTENSION

Principles of Church Growth by Wayne C. Weld and Donald A. McGavran, $4.95x paper, 400 pp.

The World Directory of Theological Education by Extension by Wayne C. Weld, $5.95x paper, 416 pp. *1976 Supplement only,* $1.95x, 64 pp.

APPLIED ANTHROPOLOGY

Becoming Bilingual: A Guide to Language Learning by Donald Larson and William A. Smalley, $5.95x paper, 426 pp.

The Church and Cultures: Applied Anthropology for the Religious Worker by Louis J. Luzbetak, $5.95x paper, 448 pp.

Customs and Cultures: Anthropology for Christian Missions by Eugene A. Nida, $3.95x paper, 322 pp.

Manual of Articulatory Phonetics by William A. Smalley, $4.95x paper, 522 pp.

Message and Mission: The Communication of the Christian Faith by Eugene A. Nida, $3.95x paper, 254 pp.

Readings in Missionary Anthropology edited by William A. Smalley, $5.95x paper, 384 pp.

Tips on Taping: Language Recording in the Social Sciences by Wayne and Lonna Dickerson, $4.95x paper, 208 pp.

REFERENCE

An American Directory of Schools and Colleges Offering Missionary Courses edited by Glenn Schwartz, $5.95x paper, 266 pp.

The Means of World Evangelization: Missiological Education at the Fuller School of World Mission edited by Alvin Martin, $9.95 paper, 544 pp.